Incredible Catholic America

Incredible Catholic America

Smallest, Tallest, Oldest, Oddest

Marion Amberg

Our Sunday Visitor
Huntington, Indiana

Nihil Obstat
Msgr. Michael Heintz, Ph.D.
Censor Librorum

Imprimatur
✠ Kevin C. Rhoades
Bishop of Fort Wayne-South Bend
December 23, 2024

The *Nihil Obstat* and *Imprimatur* are official declarations that a book is free from doctrinal or moral error. It is not implied that those who have granted the *Nihil Obstat* and *Imprimatur* agree with the contents, opinions, or statements expressed.

30 29 28 27 26 25 1 2 3 4 5 6 7 8 9

Our Sunday Visitor Publishing Division
Our Sunday Visitor, Inc.
200 Noll Plaza
Huntington, IN 46750
www.osv.com
1-800-348-2440

ISBN: 978-1-63966-102-2 (Inventory No. T2830)
1. RELIGION—Christianity—Catholic.
2. RELIGION—Christian Living—General.
3. TRAVEL—Special Interest—Religious.
eISBN: 978-1-63966-103-9
LCCN: 2024949854

Cover design: Tyler Ottinger
Interior design: Amanda Falk
Cover art: Adobe stock
Interior art: Christina Van Hecke, www.christinavanhecke.com

PRINTED IN THE UNITED STATES OF AMERICA

To all the historians, docents, archivists, journalists, and others — professional and amateur alike — who strive to keep the stories and legends of Catholic America alive. Without your dedication and keen interest in our forebears, much of our Catholic heritage would be lost to history. Because you preserve the faith of our fathers, our faith is living still. And our hearts beat high with joy whenever we hear these glorious stories of old!

CONTENTS

INTRODUCTION

Who was the first American president married by a Catholic priest? John F. Kennedy, right? Wrong! Where is the country's oldest reference to the Blessed Mother? (Think Vikings.) Which American priest declared venerable can boast a vial of blood that's still liquid? (He's the envy of Saint Januarius.) Where is the world's largest rosary collection? (Hint: It's not in the Vatican.) Which bishop was the first to wear a wig? Who is the youngest American up for sainthood? Where is America's only drive-through Stations of the Cross? How did the country's oldest religious folk art begin?

The answers to these questions are just the beginning of the incredible facts, trivia, people, and lore in Catholic America. From Maine to Hawaii, the Bering Strait to the Gulf of Mexico, the United States of America abounds in Catholic trivia. Some trivia is regional, such as "Muskrat Fridays" in Downriver Michigan or the "Shoe Shrines" in the American Southwest. Other trivia is one of a kind: How many churches can boast a sauerkraut stone as a building stone? A North Dakota church can.

Where did the "War of the Pews" take place? Read on to find out!

Yet this book is more than a collection of random facts and trivia. It also presents vignettes of heroic men and women who stood in the gap for the fledging American Catholic Church. (One priest in Maine was tarred and feathered by the anti-Catholic Know-Nothing Party.) Other vignettes are tales of holy men and women, including three religious whose bodies are rumored to be incorrupt. In a conversion story like no other, one New England family — father, mother, son, and four daughters — became Catholic and then all entered religious life. This book is pure Catholic and pure Americana. Inquiring minds, history buffs, journalists and media personalities, art and culinary lovers, and trivia nerds will find many somethings in these pages to tickle their fancy, including trivia questions scattered throughout to test one's own knowledge. This book also offers fun facts for students of any age (there's only one seven-syllable word in the whole book: septuagenarian). Got your curiosity up? Here's a quick exam: Which state capitol named for a saint was originally called Pig's Eye? Where do cats go to church? And who are the "three holy peas in a pod"? (The answers are in the book.)

This book even holds secrets that *Ripley's Believe It or Not* and the *Guinness Book of World Records* may not know. For instance, did you know that America's oldest Catholic immigrants are 1,700 years old? Or that Catholics living on one island in the United States travel back and forth in time? Or that Lutherans built the oldest Catholic church replica in America?

Each of the 300-plus facts and stories in this book boasts its own unique claim to fame. Smallest. Tallest. Oldest. Oddest (in a saintly sort of way). You won't find one holier-than-thou fact in the bunch. You will, however, find some tall tales, including the "Gold Rush" priest who named his first Indian converts Adam and Eve.

Can you get to heaven without knowing a lick of trivia? Of

course! But you'll have more fun on the journey (and a laugh or two) if you stop to indulge in a trivia moment here and there. Blessed are they who take delight in America's Catholic trivia — and a church mural painted by Monet.

How to Use This Book

This book is divided into five sections: Incredible Facts, Incredible Churches and Church Art, Incredible People of Faith, Incredible Trivia, and Incredible Legends and Lore. The stories in each of these five sections are presented at random. How could it be otherwise? Is the biggest church holier than the tiniest chapel? (Not in this book.) Does the Millionaire Nun override the Flying Nun? As the Good Book says, "The last will be first, and the first will be last" (Mt 20:16). Crack open this book anywhere, and you'll find loads of inspiring churches, people, and places. If you're looking for stories in a certain state or the District of Columbia, consult the Index by State. Here you'll find all fifty of our states and the District of Columbia listed in alphabetical order. Whenever possible, websites, GPS addresses, telephone numbers, and other pertinent information are given for each mention. The Index of Noted People in Catholic America is a quick reference if you're searching for a particular person or scanning for someone of unique interest.

Lending a historic feel to the book (many of the pieces are historic in nature), dozens of ink sketches capture the essence and era of a person or place. Scattered throughout the pages are Extreme Trivia Questions to test your American Catholic IQ (with answers included in a separate section at the end of the book). The questions were designed to work the brain and are difficult. If anyone can answer every question correctly, they should be canonized on the spot — and included as trivia in a future edition of this book!

Section One

INCREDIBLE FACTS

Biggest, Smallest, Oldest, and Other Fascinating Claims to Fame

What is it about facts that fascinates people? Why are we lured by the biggest, oldest, teeniest, and other bragging rights? Could it be that facts are even more fun than fiction? The first bishop of the moon thought so. Or is it because some of these facts take us into another realm: awe? As it turns out, there's lots to be awed over in Catholic America.

This section on incredible facts unveils dozens of Catholic record setters across the land — from the oldest cathedral (there are two "oldest cathedrals" in the United States, in fact), to the country's first basilica, to a church you can't attend. Don't even try to pick up the largest rosary! The country's Highest Mass is the real Rocky Mountain High. Get stuck on the

World's Largest Stamp Ball and you won't make it to the Biggest Last Supper.

Ready?

The procession of incredible facts is about to begin.

World's Largest Rosary Collection

If you prayed every bead of the Don Brown Rosary Collection, housed in the Columbia Gorge Museum near picturesque Stevenson, Washington, you'd be there a long, long time. Hailed by *Ripley's Believe It or Not* in 1973 as the world's largest rosary collection, the museum holds some 4,000 rosaries — that's 212,000 Hail Mary beads and 24,000 Our Father beads!

The life work of Catholic convert Donald A. Brown (1895–1975), the rosary collection is made of almost anything imaginable: glass, deer horn, olive pits, semiprecious gems, leather, even lead bullets. The smallest beads are the size of a pinhead; the largest rosary is over sixteen feet long. Perhaps the most intriguing rosary is the one given by President John F. Kennedy. When Brown learned the Massachusetts senator and naval war hero was running for president in 1960, he wrote Kennedy's campaign headquarters and asked for a rosary. He received a small wood-bead rosary reportedly used by the future president during World War II.

First Prayer to Mary

Christopher Columbus discovered America in 1492, right? "*Bah lutefisk*!" quip believers in the Kensington Runestone displayed at the Runestone Museum in Alexandria, Minnesota. According to runic writing on the graywacke slab, Vikings traversed the waterways of west-central Minnesota in 1362 — 130 years before Columbus set sail — and left a memorial carved with the letters "AVM" (*Ave Virgo Maria*).

Or is the 202-pound "artifact" an elaborate hoax contrived

by a Swedish immigrant farmer — a Lutheran, who chiseled the runes himself?

In 1898, the story runs, Olof Ohman was grubbing trees on his farm near Kensington, seventeen miles southwest of Alexandria. He found clutched in the roots of an aspen tree a large flat stone — about thirty-one inches long, sixteen inches wide, and six inches thick — with runic writing on its face and one side. Deciphered by Nordic scholars, the runes tell a bloody saga:

> Eight Goths and twenty-two Norwegians on exploration journey from Vinland over the West. We had camp by two skerries one day's journey north from this stone. We were out and fished one day. After we came home found ten men red with blood and dead. Ave Maria, save us from evil. Have ten of our party by the sea to look after our ships fourteen days' journey from this island. Year 1362.

If the runestone is indeed genuine, the "AVM" may be the first recorded prayer in America and the first reference to the Virgin Mary. It also raises many questions, including: Was a priest part of the expedition? Was Mass offered on Ohman's farmstead, now the Kensington Rune Stone Park, for the slain Vikings? Does the stone make the Alexandria area, settled by Scandinavian Lutherans, the true "Catholic birthplace of America"?

All riddles waiting to be solved.

First Bishop of the Moon

On July 20, 1969, Apollo 11 astronauts Neil Armstrong and Buzz Aldrin became the first men to walk on the moon. Bishop William D. Borders, the first bishop of the Diocese of Orlando, claimed the historic event also made him the first bishop of the moon. The bishop even let Pope St. Paul VI know of his newly expanded jurisdiction, though he boasted of just one parishioner: the man in the moon!

According to the 1917 *Code of Canon Law* in effect at the time, any newly discovered territory fell under the jurisdiction of the diocese from which the expedition was launched. Since Cape Canaveral, the launching site of Apollo 11, was in Brevard County and part of the Diocese of Orlando, Borders technically became the first bishop of the moon. The Diocese of Orlando has been over the moon ever since.

First Basilica

The Basilica of Saint Mary in downtown Minneapolis, Minnesota, winged its way into the record books. Designated America's first basilica in 1926, the spectacular Beaux-Arts temple is decked in angels — more than 500 of them. They appear in stained glass, steel, marble, bronze, and plaster. Six angels, wood carved in Italy in 1912, each sport a different face and hairstyle. Everywhere you look, angels — not to mention angels unaware — are keeping an eye out, including archangels Jophiel, Uriel, and Chamuel.

Designed by French native Emmanuel Louis Masqueray, the 1908 granite basilica was destined for greatness — and fun trivia. The basilica campus was once home to a zoo and fish market owned by Robert "Fish" Jones (the fish is an ancient Christian symbol). At 200 feet tall, the copper-clad dome is taller than the Statue of Liberty (without the pedestal), Niagara Falls, and the Colosseum in Rome.

Extreme Trivia
QUESTION 1

I am the first American of the Catholic Ruthenian-Byzantine Rite to be declared Blessed, and my beatification was the first held on American soil. My first documented miracle was a real eye-opener: My intercession helped heal an eight-year-old boy, legally blind, of juvenile macular degeneration. Who am I?

First Approved Marian Apparition

If Adele Brise had not heeded the advice of her confessor back in Belgium, the National Shrine of Our Lady of Champion in Wisconsin might not be here today. When Adele's parents decided that the family should immigrate to America, the twenty-four-year-old felt conflicted. At the time of her first Communion, Adele and several girlfriends had promised Our Lady that they would enter a convent in Champion, Belgium, and devote their lives as foreign missionaries. If she moved to America with her family, Adele would be unable to keep her commitment.

Adele sought the advice of her confessor. "Obey your parents and go to America," he counseled. "If God wills it, you will become a sister there." In 1855, the Brise family immigrated to Wisconsin and settled near Robinsonville (now called Champion). Just four years later, in October 1859, Our Lady appeared three times to Adele between two trees — a maple and a hem-

lock. The "Lady in White" asked Adele to "gather the children in this wild country and teach them what they should know for salvation." Her childhood vow of missionary work was coming to pass.

Erected in 1941, Our Lady's chapel sits on the apparition site between the two trees. On December 8, 2010, Bishop David L. Ricken of the Diocese of Green Bay proclaimed Adele's apparitions to be authentic and true. The National Shrine of Our Lady of Champion is the first and only Church-approved Marian apparition site in the United States.

Miniature Heaven

A little man, Brother Joseph Zoettl, OSB, created the biggest "smaller-than-life" tourist attraction in America: the Ave Maria Grotto at St. Bernard Abbey in Cullman, Alabama. Beginning around 1912 until 1958, Zoettl crafted 125 miniatures of famous holy places and historic monuments from junk. The dome of St. Peter's Basilica in Rome came from an old bird cage. Toilet float balls are said to cap the twin domes of a cathedral replica. Railroad spikes, cold cream jars, costume jewelry, broken plates, and even test tubes were put into service.

The monk, who was hunchbacked as a result of an injury, "shrank" the Statue of Liberty, Rome's Colosseum, the Bethlehem Cave, Noah's Ark, the Alamo, and the Tower of Babel. A pilgrimage around the world in just four acres, the tiny replicas also include the Leaning Tower of Pisa, German castles, and even the abbey's power station, where the folk artist worked shoveling coal.

Unlike the miniatures that line a wooded hillside path, the Ave Maria Grotto itself is bigger than life. Nearly three stories high, three stories wide, and three stories deep, Mary's grotto is a wonder to behold. The faux stalactites were fashioned from chunks of marble and look like they've been here since the beginning of time.

Oldest Little Flower Shrine

You'd think the world's oldest shrine to the Little Flower (St. Thérèse of Lisieux) would be in France. Wrong! Try Rhode Island. St. Theresa of the Child Jesus Church and Shrine of the Little Flower at Harrisville was formed just four months after the French Carmelite nun was beatified in April 1923. ("Theresa" was the American spelling of her name at the time.) Construction of the Basilica of Sainte-Thérèse at Lisieux, France, commenced in 1929 — four years after her canonization.

As if to emphasize Saint Thérèse's "Little Way" of love, the world's premier Little Flower shrine is located in the littlest state in the Union.

Biggest Last Supper

How big was the Last Supper table? Was it twenty-two feet long? That's the length of the wood-carved Last Supper scene at Trinity Heights Queen of Peace Shrine in Sioux City, Iowa. Modeled after da Vinci's celebrated painting, Iowa's Last Supper is famous in its own right. Woodcarver Gerald Traufler of Le Mars, Iowa, recruited friends and relatives — even his wife, Arlene — to don priests' albs and pose as the apostles. Some "Iowa Apostles" sport hairstyles and sideburns of the day. Which apostle did Arlene model? Think "Beloved."

Traufler carved individual, life-size statues of Jesus and the apostles, each weighing between 200 and 300 pounds, except for James and Andrew. The heavyweights of the bunch, their combined statue registers a hefty 550 pounds. Seven years in the carving (1986–1993), the two-ton masterpiece is the biggest Catholic Last Supper in the country and one of few such carvings in the world.

Padre Pio Miracle Shrine

In 1968, Mrs. Vera Calandra of Pennsylvania brought her two-year-old daughter, Vera Marie, to San Giovanni Rotondo, Italy, for Padre Pio's prayers. Born with congenital defects of the urinary tract, Vera Marie's bladder had to be surgically removed. Her days were numbered. As the Capuchin friar placed his stigmatic hands on the girl's head, Mrs. Calandra promised God to tell the world of Padre Pio's greatness if Vera Marie lived. Back home in Pennsylvania, the little girl was again x-rayed by doctors. They found a new bladder growing where her diseased one had been taken out!

Padre Pio died September 23, 1968, just weeks after blessing Vera Marie, and was canonized in 2002. True to her word, Mrs. Calandra and her husband, Harry, founded the National Centre for Padre Pio at Barto, Pennsylvania. Designed to resemble Padre Pio's friary at San Giovanni Rotondo, the Centre holds the world's largest collection of Pio relics outside Italy, including the very confession box where he heard the confessions of women.

Oldest Outdoor Way of the Cross

It's a penitential climb up the Outdoor Way of the Cross at St. Donatus, Iowa, believed the first of its kind in the nation. Dating from 1861, the Way — fourteen brick alcoves with framed lithographs detailing Christ's journey to Calvary — runs switchback up the steep hill behind St. Donatus Church. Atop the hill, the Pietà Chapel, a copy of Chapelle du Bildchen at Vianden, Luxembourg, holds a statue of Mary with her crucified Son. Be careful where you tread, however. Animals are also known to make the Way and leave calling cards.

War of the Pews

Established in 1841, Saint Augustine Catholic Church in New Orleans, Louisiana, is billed as the first Catholic church for people of color in America. But it's the "War of the Pews" that makes this historic landmark on the Louisiana African American Trail such a noted attraction. In 1842, a few months before the church dedication on October 9, free people of color began buying pews for their families to sit in (this was during an era of pew fees). When white Catholics got wind of this, they started a campaign to buy more pews than the Black Catholics. The War of the Pews was on!

The free people of color won the pew war, buying three pews to every one purchased by the whites. The free people of color also bought all the pews in the two side aisles and gave those pews to enslaved Blacks for their exclusive worship space — a first in American history. The mix of "free pews, white pews, and slave pews" resulted in the country's most integrated church for decades to come. The warring pews still seat parishioners today.

For Goodness Saints!

If there's a heaven on earth, it must be in northern New Mexico. Not a day passes here that a new saint isn't made. Oh, these saints aren't being canonized; they've already earned their halos. Rather, they're being sanded, painted, carved, punched, and polished to perfection. But then, spiritual beauty is in the eye of the *santeros* — the saint-makers.

And when these saints go marching in, the public comes out ... at the Traditional Spanish Market held annually on the Historic Santa Fe Plaza in Santa Fe the last full weekend in July. Hundreds of *santeros* display a litany of saints — from Agnes to Ysidro. Can't decide? There's always Saint Jude, patron of hopeless causes.

A Spanish colonial tradition, saint-making dates from the 1700s and is the oldest religious folk art form in the United States. Lacking statues and crucifixes in the outback missions, tradition holds, itinerant Franciscan padres taught the colonists to carve *santos* and *Cristos* and paint *retablos* (images on wood or animal hides) to adorn the adobe churches and help keep the Faith alive. Three centuries later, descendants of the original *santeros* — and "*santeros*-come-lately" — still use straw (poor man's gold) and tin (poor's man's silver) to craft their saints. The collectible artworks often depict red drapes drawn back as though revealing mysteries of the Faith.

Terror of Demons

Around the noon hour on October 23, 1970, fifty priests were concelebrating Mass at the Virgen de San Juan Shrine at San

Juan, Texas, when a deranged pilot deliberately flew a small plane into the church. Miraculously, all fifty priests and the worshipers in the pews escaped before the building exploded into a fireball. Thankfully, no children in the adjacent school cafeteria were harmed. The Blessed Sacrament and the three-foot Virgen de San Juan statue were rescued, unsinged.

What was meant for harm that horrible day turned into magnanimous good beyond imagination. In 1980, a new 55,000-square-foot shrine was dedicated. Seating over 2,000, the Basilica of Our Lady of San Juan del Valle National Shrine averages 20,000 visitors per weekend — more than one million pilgrims a year.

Nothing about this shrine is minuscule. Greeting pilgrims is a massive exterior mosaic of Christ presenting his mother, Our Lady of San Juan, to the Rio Grande Valley. A terror of demons, the outdoor holy water plaza is one of the world's largest holy water fonts, if not the largest. The font, with multiple spigots, is so big it holds enough holy water to sprinkle the entire Diocese of Brownsville. This is Texas, after all.

Largest Ball of Stamps

Boys Town, Nebraska, is stuck on stamps. It began in the 1930s when Boys Town founder Father Edward J. Flanagan (1886–1948) saw stamp collecting as an educational hobby for boys in his care. In 1953, someone came up with the idea of creating a stamp ball. The boys began pasting layers upon layers of canceled stamps around a core (tradition holds it was a golf ball). The World's Largest Ball of Stamps grew and grew until it reached its current size in 1955 — a 600-pound ball, thirty-two inches in diameter. Estimated number of stamps used: 4,655,000.

Featured in *Ripley's Believe It or Not*, the biggest stamp ball is displayed in the Boys Town Visitor Center. In 1986, the United

States Post Office issued a four-cent commemorative stamp to mark Flanagan's one-hundredth birthday. The Servant of God who encouraged stamp collecting had now become a collectible item himself.

"First Green Basilica"

"Store up treasures in heaven," Jesus exhorts us in Matthew 6:20. So, why do the doorknobs of the Basilica of Saint Josaphat in Milwaukee, Wisconsin, bear the insignia of the United States Department of the Treasury? Because this basilica is "green" — made from repurposed material. When Father Wilhelm Grutza began erecting the majestic Polish church in 1897, he learned the United States Post Office and Customs House in Chicago was slated for demolition. He bought the building for $20,000 and had the contents — carved stone, wooden doors, light fixtures, ornamental bronze railings, and doorknobs — dismantled and shipped on 500 railroad cars to Milwaukee.

And it thereby happened that the treasures of the United States Post Office building became the treasures of heavenly Saint Josaphat's, a smaller version of St. Peter's Basilica in Rome. (St. Peter's can't boast of treasury doorknobs, however.) Sometimes called an "ignored wonder of the world," Saint Josaphat's was named the country's third basilica in 1929. It's also the "First Green Basilica."

Highest Mass in America

There are High Masses and Low Masses. Then there's the highest Mass in America at the Church of the Annunciation of the Blessed Virgin Mary in Leadville, Colorado. Sitting at an elevation of 10,430 feet above sea level, the Rocky Mountain church is touted as having the highest church spire in the land. It's said the lofty spire — 150 feet high — is so high that angels stop here for "wing breaks."

Founded by Irish miners in 1879, the nearly two-mile-high church witnessed the 1886 wedding of Margaret Tobin and James J. Brown. Mrs. Brown later went down in history as the "Unsinkable Molly Brown" when she survived the sinking of the *Titanic* in 1912.

Lucky Saint Patrick

In the late 1850s, Father Bernard Patrick McMenomy made application for a post office for the little Irish settlement of St. Marysville, in extreme northeastern Missouri. But Missouri already had a town with a similar name, so McMenomy decided to rename the settlement Saint Patrick. It was a stroke of luck. Saint Patrick, Missouri, is the world's only town with a post office named for Ireland's patron saint.

Saint Patrick got lucky again in 1935, when Father Francis O'Duignan, the new pastor, rolled into town. The Irish native dreamed of erecting a shrine to Patrick — and where better than in Saint Patrick? It took him twenty-two years to build the stone church. Modeled after the Church of the Four Masters in Donegal, Ireland, the Shrine of Saint Patrick is famous for its Celtic design with round bell tower and stained glass windows inspired by the Book of Kells. During the shrine dedication on March 17, 1957 — Saint Patrick's Day, of course — O'Duignan had a pilot fly over and drop shamrocks on the town. The priest also started the shrine's annual fundraiser: Paddy Day greetings stamped with a green shamrock cachet that reads "Saint Patrick, MO. The Only One in the World."

Oldest Chapel Is Older than America

America's oldest chapel isn't American. It's French! Not only that, but St. Joan of Arc Chapel at Marquette University in Milwaukee, Wisconsin, is 350 years older than America itself. How did the little French chapel come to the Heartland of America? It's a story of many miles.

In 1926, Gertrude Hill Gavin, daughter of railroad tycoon James J. Hill, acquired the Chapelle de St. Martin de Seyssuel, erected c. 1420 in the village of Chasse, near Lyon, France. Gavin shipped the chapel stones, all numbered, to her Long Island estate in New York — a French Renaissance château, also shipped from France and rebuilt. A devotee of St. Joan of Arc (1412–1431), Gavin renamed the Gothic chapel for the young French heroine burned at the stake.

Gavin died in 1961, and the estate came into the hands of

tractor magnate Marc B. Rojtman and his wife, Lillian. Just days before they were scheduled to move in, a fire gutted the château, but the chapel was spared as if by a miracle. St. Joan of Arc Chapel was donated to Marquette University, shipped again stone by stone, and reassembled a second time.

But there's one chapel stone that stands out among all others. When Gavin bought the oratory, now 600 years old, she also acquired a thirteenth-century altar and the "Joan of Arc Stone." It's said the soldier-saint prayed on this very stone and then kissed it before going off to war. Why the stone feels colder to the touch than the other stones around it, nobody knows.

Solitary Monastery

Don't even think about visiting the Charterhouse of the Transfiguration on Mount Equinox near Arlington, Vermont. The Charterhouse — the only Carthusian monastery in North America — is never open to the public. The monks, followers of Saint Bruno, who founded the Carthusian Order in 1084, are solitaires and spend up to nineteen hours a day alone in their cells, where they pray, work, take meals, and sleep. The solitaires gather in community three times daily for Mass and other prayers.

Opened in 1970, the monastery, nestled in a 7,000-acre spread, is visible from Mount Equinox Skyline Drive — a five-mile, hairpin toll road that winds and winds and winds to the Saint Bruno Scenic Viewing Center at the top.

City of Firsts

St. Augustine, Florida, is a city of historic firsts. On September 8, 1565 — feast of the Nativity of the Blessed Virgin Mary — Admiral Pedro Menéndez de Avilés and some 800 Spanish colonists aboard a fleet of ships came ashore, and Father Francisco López de Mendoza Grajales offered the first parish Mass at the first permanent European settlement in the US. The first Mass also marked

St. Augustine as the birthplace of Christianity in America — fifty-five years before the Pilgrims landed at Plymouth Rock in 1620.

Menéndez called the site *Nombre de Dios* (Name of God) and put López in charge of America's first parish (today's Cathedral Basilica of St. Augustine). In the early 1600s, settlers enshrined a small statue of *Nuestra Señora de La Leche y Buen Parto* (Our Lady of the Milk and Happy Delivery) in the mission chapel, making it the country's first Marian shrine. It's said that Our Lady of La Leche, patroness of couples trying to conceive and of problem pregnancies, has been busy delivering miracle babies across our land ever since.

Dubbed "America's Most Sacred Acre," the historic site is known today as the National Shrine of Our Lady of La Leche at Mission Nombre de Dios.

Painting of Biblical Proportions

The list of movie stars buried in Forest Lawn Memorial Park at Glendale, California, reads like a who's who — but the real star of the memorial park is *The Crucifixion*, a painting of biblical proportions. The work of Polish Catholic artist Jan Styka (1858–1925), the panoramic masterpiece measures a staggering 195 feet in length and forty-five feet in height. The saga of the country's largest religious painting began around 1894 and is as big as the artwork itself.

After traveling to Jerusalem to sketch the city where Jesus was crucified, with a stopover in Rome to have Pope Leo XIII bless his palette and brushes, Styka returned home to Poland to begin painting the 8,775-square-foot spectacle — his vision of what happened on Calvary just before the crucifixion took place. It's said the painting took six years to complete. When it was displayed in Europe, crowds were bowled over by its majestic splendor. Then, Styka was invited to exhibit the artwork at the 1904 World's Fair in St. Louis, Missouri.

When his ship docked in New York, Styka learned that he had been misled; no facility at the World's Fair was large enough to hold the giant crucifixion scene. Making matters even worse, custom officials seized the painting for nonpayment of duty. Styka, who had exhausted his resources traveling to America, couldn't ransom the artwork and was forced to return home without it. He never saw his masterpiece again.

Decades passed, and the confiscated painting wound up in Chicago where it languished in a series of warehouses. *The Crucifixion* remained "lost" until 1943, when Hubert L. Eaton, founder of Forest Lawn, and his colleagues found the painting in the basement of the Chicago Civic Opera House, wrapped around a telephone pole. Eaton, a Baptist, purchased the painting and erected the Hall of Crucifixion at Forest Lawn specifically to display the epic Catholic artwork. The first showing took place on Good Friday, 1951.

Beginning with the City of Jerusalem at the right, the painting — more than twice as wide as an IMAX screen — pans to the center where a life-size Jesus, in his final moments before execution, is enveloped in a heavenly light. He is surrounded by the Blessed Mother, Mary Magdalene, Simon of Cyrene, and a thousand extras — characters from every station in life — as they might have looked and acted on that day. The bearded Styka is there too, portrayed as Saul.

Extreme Trivia
QUESTION 2

A colony of German Catholics founded the hamlet of __ ville, Kansas, in the 1880s and named it for a then-living pope. Who was the pope?

Biggest and Smallest Dioceses

How well do you know your American Catholic geography? Which diocese is the largest areawise? (It's bigger than Texas.) Which diocese is the smallest?

Founded in 1853, the Diocese of Brooklyn, New York, is the smallest diocese in land size. Serving the boroughs of Brooklyn and Queens, the diocese covers 180 square miles and is roughly one-sixth the size of Rhode Island, the smallest state at 1,214 square miles. As small as it is, the diocese serves 1.3 million Catholics at 176 parishes and offers Masses in 26 languages.

The biggest state in the Union, Alaska, claims the biggest diocese. The Diocese of Fairbanks was created in 1962, just three years after Alaska became the 49th state. Spanning 409,849 square miles, the mission diocese covers nearly two-thirds of Alaska and is roughly 34 percent larger than the State of Texas (268,597 square miles).

Only nine of the forty-six parishes in the Diocese of Fairbanks are on the highway road system. Depending on the season, clergy and other diocesan personnel travel to parishes "off the road" by plane, boat, or snowmachine. Getting stuck in bad weather is akin to getting stuck in traffic, except it might be days before the weather changes.

World's Largest Tile Mural

During morning Mass on New Year's Eve, 1956, worshipers at the Cathedral of Saint Joseph in Hartford, Connecticut, smelled smoke. By that afternoon, the majestic neo-Gothic structure was a smoldering ruin. Archbishop Henry J. O'Brien had one stipulation for the architects of a new cathedral: It must be a contemporary design for contemporary times. Consecrated in 1962, the Cathedral of Saint Joseph is not only contemporary but massive — in size and spirit.

Built of reinforced concrete and clad in limestone, the cathedral rises 281 feet and is three-quarters of a football field long. The 26 stained glass windows are each nearly 70 feet high by fourteen feet wide. (It's hard to ignore these stained glass sermonettes!) The cathedral centerpiece, however, is the world's largest ceramic tile mural. Titled *Christ in Glory*, the mural — with a twenty-nine-foot figure of Our Lord — spans 40 by 80 feet and is composed of 1,152 individual sections. It took 1 year to assemble.

Largest Catholic Megachurch

How many worshipers can the largest Catholic parish church in America hold? At least 3,200 — more people than the population of many small towns. Dedicated in 2023, St. Charles Borromeo Church in Visalia, California, encompasses 34,000 square feet and serves 14,000 registered families. The parking lot alone holds nearly 900 parking spaces.

Designed in California mission style, the megachurch showcases some impressive artworks too. The eight-sided dome with star-studded sky, based on photos taken with the Hubble telescope, whisks Mass goers to heaven, while an enormous floor-to-ceiling sanctuary painting keeps them grounded in faith. Set in the San Joaquin Valley, the painting, with rolling fields of orchard trees and plump Holstein cows, pays tribute to God's bounty and the local agricultural industry. Why the "holy cows"? Because Visalia is located in Tulare County, the dairy capital of California.

"Greatest Jigsaw Puzzle"

The Ancient Spanish Monastery at North Miami Beach, Florida — considered the oldest building in the Western Hemisphere — lives up to its name. Nearly 900 years old, the Cistercian cloister was constructed from 1133 to 1141, near the small town of Sacramenia in northern Spain. For seven centuries, monks walked these hallowed corridors, saturating the very stones with prayer. During the First Carlist War in the 1830s, the cloister was seized, sold, and turned into a granary.

In 1925, newspaper tycoon William Randolph Hearst bought the medieval monastery and outbuildings. The structures were taken down, stone by stone, packed with hay into 11,000 numbered crates, and shipped to America. Getting the crates past customs was another story. Because the stones were packed in hay that was possibly contaminated with hoof-and-mouth disease, US officials quarantined the shipment. The crates were emptied, the hay filling removed and burned, and the 35,000-plus stones randomly stuffed back into the wooden boxes.

Adding to the misery, Hearst fell upon hard times, and the crates landed in a New York warehouse for over two decades. In 1951, two entrepreneurs acquired the mountain of stones. But putting the monastery back together again would take nineteen months and $1.5 million (over $18 million today). According to a 1954 article in *TIME* magazine, the master mason overseeing the project called it "the greatest jigsaw puzzle in history." Some stones never found their rightful places.

While the Ancient Spanish Monastery now serves as an Episcopal church, it remains a popular historic Catholic attraction. Where else in America can you see a medieval bell (the bellringer is a little metal monk on a rope), a fourteenth-century marble frieze of the Magi worshiping the Baby Jesus, a chapter house, and a medieval shrine to Mary in one place?

From Cornfield Hospital to World Renown

When Mother Alfred Moes, OSF, opened Saint Marys Hospital in a cornfield near Rochester, Minnesota, in 1889, it should have failed from the start. Dr. W. W. Mayo was seventy years old, and neither of his young sons, Will and Charlie (both doctors), had any hospital experience. Greener still were the nurses — Franciscan sisters trained as schoolteachers and not accustomed to seeing bodies and blood. Anti-Catholic sentiment didn't help matters: Townsfolk were suspicious of the partnership between the Protestant Mayos and the Catholic sisters. Yet with scalpel and prayer and a credo that "the needs of the patient come first," the twenty-seven-bed "cornfield hospital" evolved into the world-famous Mayo Clinic today.

World's Largest Grotto

Father Paul Mathias Dobberstein's word was rock solid. Falling deathly ill with double pneumonia in 1897, the German immigrant begged Mother Mary's intercession and vowed to build her a grotto if he lived. Keeping his promise, he not only erected Mary's Grotto but a composite of nine separate grottoes. Covering a city block, the Shrine of the Grotto of the Redemption at West Bend, Iowa, tells in stone — from the Garden of Eden to the Crucifixion — the greatest story ever told. The grotto's highest peak is Golgotha, a forty-foot-tall stone mountain.

All that glitters in the world's largest man-made grotto is not fool's gold. Because Iowa is hardly a geological hotbed, the rockhound-spelunking Dobberstein traveled to the Black Hills, the American Southwest, Arkansas, and other points in search of building material. Some 100 train cars of petrified wood, fossils, stalactites and stalagmites, agates as big as a person's head, shells, quartz of every color, barite roses (rocks shaped like roses), semiprecious stones, mud balls, and more were used to construct the shrine, heralded as the "Eighth Wonder of the World."

Longest Church Art Project

The longest-running church art project in America? The dazzling mosaics adorning the Cathedral Basilica of St. Louis in St. Louis, Missouri. Created by twenty different artists, the mosaics — covering a colossal 83,000 square feet — began in 1912 and were completed seventy-six years later, in 1988. A whopping 41.5 million pieces of glass tesserae, in over 7,000 colors, portray myriad figures and events, from Elijah being taken up to heaven in a fiery chariot to the Last Supper (two Last Supper mosaics, in fact) to missionaries on the American frontier.

But it's the artistic details that make the mosaics so compelling and thought-provoking. What do the hourglasses with wings portray? (The fleeing nature of time.) Who is the Black Robe wearing an embroidered buckskin jacket? (Jesuit missionary Father Pierre-Jean De Smet.) Which saint is carrying his head (with a halo) to Jesus? (John the Baptist.) What do the five different styles of boats represent? (Modes of water transportation over the millennia.) Why does St. Rose Philippine Duchesne have a fractured halo? (She was on her way to sainthood but not yet canonized when the mosaic was installed.)

Church on Top of the World

Wear a parka and long johns if you want to attend Mass on top of the world. Boasting the world's northernmost Catholic church, Saint Patrick's at Utqiagvik (formerly Barrow), Alaska, is located 330 miles above the Arctic Circle. The daily low temperature dips below freezing 324 days of the year. Folks here also experience a yearly death and resurrection of sorts. Between November 18 and January 24, the sun does not rise, and the town plunges into darkness. Between May 10 and August 2, the sun does not set.

A Baptismal High

Get baptized at the Cathedral of the Immaculate Conception in Portland, Maine, a Gothic-style beauty opened in 1869, and you'll already have one foot in heaven. The baptismal font is over thirteen feet tall and five feet in diameter! Crowning the dome of the elaborate white marble font, inspired by a font in Italy's Cathedral of Pietrasanta, is a cross and statue of the Risen Christ. Marble panels around the font hold bronze statues of Jeremiah, Ezekiel, Daniel, and Zechariah, all messianic messengers. The bronze front door depicts John the Baptist baptizing Jesus, the Messiah.

But don't worry about climbing the century-old font — believed the country's tallest — to receive the waters of eternal life. The font stands inside a small immersion pool of white marble.

Tallest Church Cross

Many churches are cruciform (in the shape of a cross), but the stunningly beautiful Chapel of the Holy Cross at Sedona, Arizona, was built *on* the cross. Ascending between twin red rocks that seemingly parted like the Red Sea, a ninety-foot cross of reinforced concrete — the country's tallest church cross — serves both structural and spiritual functions. The chapel even began with a "sign of the cross."

In 1932, while gazing on the newly completed Empire State Building in New York City, Catholic sculptor Marguerite Brunswig Staude saw an image of a tall cross that seemed to superimpose itself on the building. "What an idea for a church!" she wrote. The image would haunt her until it became reality. The Chapel of the Holy Cross, with floor-to-ceiling vistas of the surrounding red rock landscape, was completed in 1956. Even nature bows to this cross: One red rock formation resembles the Madonna and Child, another, praying nuns.

Oldest Crucifix

In the 1920s, an importer brought a humongous wooden crucifix, hand carved in Spain, to the US with the intent of selling it to a Chicago museum. But this Christ didn't want to hang in a museum, and the polychrome crucifix, between 600 and 800 years old, eventually took up residence at St. Augustine Cathedral in Tucson, Arizona. Known as the Crucifix of Pamplona, it stands seventeen feet tall and weighs one ton. Believed to be the country's oldest crucifix, it's also one of the most spiritually moving. The nails in Christ's hands and feet are highly visible, his wounds and lashes bloody and graphic.

First Interracial Monastery

In the late 1930s, Mother Mary of Jesus, prioress of the cloistered Dominican Sisters of the Perpetual Rosary in Catonsville, Maryland, had a vision: a race riot of angry mobs clubbing each other. Suddenly, the scene changed. The same mobs were now kneeling, their weapons replaced with rosaries. On a distant hill was a monastery with nuns of all races praying the Rosary, their arms outstretched in the form of a cross. Before the prioress died in 1939, she confided her vision to Sister Mary Dominic of the Rosary, another Catonsville nun.

When a Black woman was denied entrance to the Catonsville monastery because of her race, Sister Mary Dominic of the Rosary and Sister Mary of the Child Jesus decided the time had come to bring the prioress's vision to reality. They began a letter-writing campaign to bishops, seeking permission to begin an interracial monastery in their diocese. Time and again, the nuns were denied, just like the Black woman at their own monastery. Finally, Bishop (later Archbishop) Thomas J. Toolen of Mobile helped the nuns begin an integrated monastery at Marbury, Alabama, even though segregation was still the law in the Deep South.

Set on a hill just like the vision foretold, the Dominican Monastery of St. Jude, the country's first interracial monastery, opened in 1944. Clad in white habits with black veils, these nuns are "warring angels." Attached to their black belts, where knights of old would carry a sword, is a rosary — their weapon against violence in the world.

Oldest Corpus Christi Procession

Holy Family Church in Oldenburg, Indiana, boasts not only the nation's oldest parish Corpus Christi procession but quite possibly the loudest. Dating from 1846, the procession has changed little over the years. Cross and flag bearers lead the entourage through the German village, with "shooters" bringing up the rear. As the priest blesses the throngs at each outdoor altar with the monstrance, the shooters salute the Eucharistic king with a salvo of gun blasts. "The Father." Bang! "The Son." Bang! "The Holy Spirit." Bang!

Remarkably, the parish hasn't missed a Corpus Christi procession in 180 years — not during the Civil War, the two world wars, or the two pandemics of 1918 and 2019.

Largest Catholic Pilgrimage

It was the largest Catholic pilgrimage in American history and possibly the world. During Pentecost weekend in 2024, caravans of pilgrims from the four corners of the country began walking with the Eucharistic Lord in procession. Their destination: the National Eucharistic Congress in Indianapolis, Indiana (held July 17–21). The Congress was part of a three-year, nationwide Eucharistic revival.

Forming a gigantic, rugged cross on a map of the United States, the four arms of the National Eucharistic Pilgrimage stretched 6,500 miles and traversed twenty-seven states and sixty-five dioceses. The northern arm of the cross originated at the headwaters of the Mississippi River near Park Rapids, Minnesota. The southern arm commenced in South Texas at Brownsville. The eastern arm of the cross departed from New Haven, Connecticut, and the western arm from San Francisco, California.

Four routes. Hundreds of thousands of pilgrims. Onlookers blessed as Our Lord passed them by: multitudes.

America's First Lady

Who's the first First Lady of America? No, not Martha, wife of first president George Washington. The First Lady is Mary, the Mother of God. When Columbus sailed to America in 1492, his flagship was christened the *Santa María* (Holy Mary). When the English ships the *Ark* and the *Dove*, carrying both Protestant and Catholic colonists, landed at St. Clements Island in the Potomac River on March 25, 1634, the new colony was called Maryland. For Protestants, the name honored Mary, the Queen of England, and for Catholics, the Queen of Heaven.

It was Mary, the Queen of Heaven, who reigned over St. Mary's City — located on St. Mary's River on the Bay of the Mother of God (now Chesapeake Bay) — Maryland's first settlement. Even though Maryland Day commemorates the founding of Maryland, it falls on March 25, feast of the Annunciation of the Blessed Virgin Mary.

Historic First Cathedral

The Basilica of the National Shrine of the Assumption of the Blessed Virgin Mary in Baltimore, Maryland — Baltimore Basilica for short — is a record setter in American Catholic history. Dubbed America's First Cathedral, the hilltop neoclassical edifice was built between 1806 and 1821 by Bishop John Carroll, the country's first bishop, and Benjamin Henry Latrobe, famed architect of the US Capitol.

Eschewing the traditional Gothic and Romanesque architecture of European cathedrals, Carroll wanted an architectural symbol that was uniquely American and which celebrated freedom of worship under the new Constitution. For more than a century until the American Revolution, Catholics were persecuted. Priests often traveled incognito and offered clandestine Masses in homes. Some homes even had priest holes (hiding places). Pope St. John Paul II called America's First Cathedral a "worldwide symbol of religious freedom."

Many noteworthy events occurred within the cathedral's hallowed walls, including the funeral Mass for Charles Carroll of Carrollton, Bishop Carroll's cousin and the sole Catholic signer of the Declaration of Independence. In 1846, the US bishops convened at the cathedral and declared the Blessed Mother, under the title of the Immaculate Conception, patroness of America. *The Baltimore Catechism* was commissioned here in 1884.

In 1959, the Cathedral of Mary Our Queen in Baltimore — a much grander structure — supplanted the basilica as cathedral of the Archdiocese of Baltimore. But nothing can take away the basilica's historic claim as America's First Cathedral.

The "Other" First Cathedral

Not to split cathedral hairs with America's First Cathedral in Baltimore, but the Cathedral-Basilica of Saint Louis King of France in New Orleans, Louisiana, also vies for "first cathedral" status. In 1793, Pope Pius VI created the Diocese of Louisiana and the Floridas, with Luis Peñalver y Cárdenas of Cuba as first bishop. The Church of Saint Louis, built in 1789, rose to cathedral rank in 1794 — twenty-seven years before Baltimore's cathedral opened in 1821. Louisiana joined the United States in 1812, six years after the Baltimore cornerstone was laid.

The New Orleans cathedral, with iconic triple spires, got a major uplift in the 1850s, and little remains of the original structure. Like much of the French Quarter, the venerable cathedral has its own legends — holy spirits, at that. Père Dagobert (*Père* is French for Father) has been spotted walking the church aisles in Capuchin robe and tricorn hat, singing the Kyrie, while Père

Antoine appears during Christmas Eve Midnight Mass, a lighted candle in hand.

Eucharistic Miracle

Samuel Sutherland Cooper (1769–1843) experienced one of the first — if not the first — Eucharistic miracles in America. Born at Norfolk, Virginia, and baptized an Anglican, Cooper owned and captained a vessel, traversing the high seas in search of riches and adventure. The religious skeptic was very wealthy, extremely handsome, a splendid dancer, and the best billiard player around — until one day around 1805, when an invisible hand began shaking him vigorously. A mysterious voice said the words, "Jesus," "Water," and "Spirit."

The shaken Cooper mended his ways, converted to Catholicism in 1807, and entered St. Mary's Seminary at Baltimore, Maryland. Ordained in 1818, the new priest was assigned the following year to St. Patrick's Church in Augusta, Georgia, deep in the Protestant South. One day while hearing public denunciations of the Mass and transubstantiation, tradition holds Cooper rashly declared a miracle of the Real Presence would happen at his Mass the following Sunday.

Fear overtook the impetuous priest, and he begged God to save him and the Church from disgrace. St. Patrick's Church was crowded that Sunday; everyone had come to see Sutherland's avowed miracle. As the nervous celebrant elevated the consecrated Host, a loud shriek escaped his throat. The Host had turned to bleeding flesh!

In 1857, a new St. Patrick's Church was erected and is known today as the Church of the Most Holy Trinity. In another historic sidebar, the church's three marble altars — crafted by John P. Mullen in Baltimore — were smuggled through a Union blockade during the Civil War.

Oldest Catholic Newspaper

The country's oldest Catholic newspapers are stories in themselves. When secular newspapers in Charleston, South Carolina, refused to publish Bishop John England's letters to the editor refuting nativist attacks on the Church, he had to buy advertising space to get them printed. In 1822, England, the first ordinary of the Charleston diocese, launched the *United States Catholic Miscellany* — the country's first Catholic weekly. England wrote

Extreme Trivia
QUESTION 3

The Cathedral Basilica of St. John the Baptist in Savannah, Georgia, was erected in the late 1800s in French Gothic style. The nave ceiling is sixty-six feet high — that's over six stories tall. How many Catholic men does it take to change a light bulb in the cathedral ceiling?

many of the articles himself, sometimes under a nom de plume.

When South Carolina seceded from the Union in 1860, the *Catholic Miscellany* expunged "United States" from its nameplate. Editor and secessionist Father James A. Corcoran wrote he could no longer tolerate "those two obnoxious words." A year later, the Great Charleston Fire destroyed the newspaper's offices and printing presses, and the paper ceased publication. In 1990, Bishop David B. Thompson resurrected the diocesan paper, renaming it *The New Catholic Miscellany*. The award-winning publication is now called *The Catholic Miscellany*.

But *The Pilot*, the official publication of the Archdiocese of Boston, Massachusetts, claims the title of "America's Oldest Continuous Catholic Newspaper." Founded in 1829, the paper also sought to defend the Church against calumnies and gross misrepresentations. And like the *United States Catholic Miscellany*, the newspaper offices burned to the ground in Boston's Great Fire of 1872 and then twice more in rapid succession at new locations. Editor John Boyle O'Reilly penned, "When a fire comes to Boston nowadays, it comes looking for its friend *The Pilot*. It is evident that the fire has a rare appreciation of a good newspaper."

The Pilot's name evolved over the decades. Beginning with the awkward title of *The Jesuit or Catholic Sentinel*, other nameplates included *The United States Catholic Intelligencer*, *The Literary and Catholic Sentinel*, and *The Boston Pilot*. Today, it is simply *The Pilot*.

Largest Geographical Parish

Holy Rosary Catholic Church in Dillingham, Alaska, borders the Dillingham airport. That's where the pastor's wheels are: a Piper Cherokee Warrior II single-engine plane. The church is also the headquarters of Saint Paul Mission. Unofficially the largest geographical parish on earth, Saint Paul Mission covers 33,000 square miles in southwest Alaska, an area roughly the size of the state of Maine. Only air miles connect Dillingham — itself accessible only by air or boat — with two mission churches and some thirty native villages scattered throughout the Alaskan Bush. Village "airports" are often simply narrow dirt runways.

"Flying the Gospel to the Ends of the Earth," the mission's motto, comes at great personal risk. Saint Paul Mission founder Father James F. Kelly, a retired Navy pilot and chaplain, crashed and died in 2002 while flying to Togiak to offer Palm Sunday Mass.

Replica of a 900-Year-Old Church

Want to see a replica of a 900-year-old medieval Catholic church? Visit the Chapel of the Hills near Rapid City, South Dakota. In 1969, the Evangelical Lutheran Church in America erected the wooden chapel — an exact replica of the famous Borgund Stavkirke (stave church) at Laerdal, Norway. Constructed around 1150, the Borgund Stavkirke served as a Catholic house of worship until the Protestant Reformation in the sixteenth century.

The Chapel in the Hills is more medieval and folkloric than first meets the eye. Built in basilica style without nails (wooden dowels hold the whole structure together), the six-tiered stavkirke is surmounted by a cross, with four carved dragon

heads warding off evil. It's said the three narrow doors — one for the priest, one for the men, and one for the women — prevented people from taking the devil at their side into church.

And that was the beginning of a "Catholic stavkirke rush" in the Norwegian Midwest. Scandinavian Heritage Park at Minot, North Dakota, boasts a full-size replica of the Gol Stave Catholic Church, built around 1200 at Gol, Norway. One dragon head appears to be smiling — did he catch the devil by the tail, perhaps?

In Moorhead, Minnesota, the Hopperstad Stave Church Replica at the Hjemkomst Center is a full-scale reproduction of the twelfth-century Catholic church at Vik, Norway. A covered walkway with a window allowed the sick and lepers standing outside to receive Communion and a blessing from the priest.

Why do Scandinavian Americans find these Catholic replicas so fascinating? Perhaps because they represent the Church of their ancestral Faith.

Jesteśmy Pierwsi!

Catholics in Bigfork, Montana, don't typically speak Polish. If they did, they might say, "*Jesteśmy pierwsi!*" ("We're the first!") That's because their church is the first church in the world named for Polish Pope St. John Paul II. How did a small-town parish get such a big bragging right? Providential timing.

The parish was in the midst of building a new church when Pope John Paul II died on April 2, 2005. To honor the beloved pontiff, the parish decided to name the new church for the first-ever Slavic pope. Pope John Paul II Catholic Church was dedicated on August 21, 2005, just four months after the pope's death. As the pope's cause for canonization progressed, the church name changed, too — from Pope John Paul II Church to Blessed Pope John Paul II Church (2011) to Saint John Paul II Church (2014).

The pope-saint, who loved to hike, would feel right at home in Bigfork. The town is surrounded by mountains and the great outdoors.

Largest Good Friday Pilgrimage

On Good Friday, 1810, *Penitentes* (men dedicated to Jesus' sufferings) were performing penances on the hills around Chimayó, New Mexico, when Bernardo Abeyta saw a light coming from the ground near the Santa Cruz River. He ran to the light, dug in the dirt, and found a crucifix! Around 1815, Abeyta began erecting the Santuario de Chimayó — a small adobe chapel with four-foot-thick walls — over the hole where the crucifix was found.

Before long, pilgrims were trekking here by foot to venerate Our Lord on the cross.

They still come by foot today.

On Good Friday, tens of thousands of pilgrims line the roads to the historic village of Chimayó — a procession that extends as far as the eye can see. Parents pushing children in strollers. Boyfriends and girlfriends. Grandparents and grandchildren. Religious men and women in habits. They come from the north, the south, the east, and the west, all converging on the Santuario to commemorate Jesus' salvific death on the cross. The Good Friday walk is the largest annual religious pilgrimage in the country.

Nobody knows when the Good Friday pilgrimages began. But it's said that during World War II, New Mexican soldiers captured by the Japanese and forced to make the Bataan Death March beseeched God, "Spare our lives." In return, they promised to make the Good Friday pilgrimage to Chimayó. And they did in 1946, their first year back home. They came on crutches, in wheelchairs, and in the arms of other soldiers.

Biggest Church

It's hailed as the largest Roman Catholic church in North America (the exterior is 459 feet long — ninety-nine feet longer than a football field) and is among the ten largest churches in the world. It's neither a cathedral nor a parish church; every American Catholic is a member. Byzantine-Romanesque in design, the superstructure was constructed (1920–1959) entirely of stone, brick, tile, and mortar — without steel structural beams, framework, or columns. Adorning the massive interior are 93,845 square feet of mosaic artworks; the Trinity Dome mosaic alone employed 14 million pieces of hand-chiseled Venetian glass.

Where are you?

Welcome to the Basilica of the National Shrine of the Immaculate Conception in Washington, DC. Also called America's Catholic Church or simply Mary's Shrine, the magnificent temple honors the Blessed Mother, patroness of the United States, under the title of the Immaculate Conception. More than eighty chapels and oratories reflect the country's ethnic Marian traditions, including Mary Queen of Ireland, Our Lady of China, Our Lady of Altötting (Bavaria, Germany), Our Lady of Lebanon, Our Lady of Africa, Our Lady of La Vang (Vietnam), Our Lady of Pompeii (Italy), and Our Lady of Vailankanni (India).

Disputed Church

The Basilica of the Sacred Heart of Jesus in Hanover, Pennsylvania, stands in disputed territory, as attested by two coats of arms in the vestibule. One side of the vestibule holds a portion of William Penn's coat of arms, the other side a portion of Lord Baltimore's coat of arms. The original land grants given to each man by kings of England overlapped. German Catholics claimed the land belonged to Pennsylvania, while English Catholics said it was Maryland territory. The boundary dispute eventually led to the creation of the Mason–Dixon Line, the border between Pennsylvania and Maryland — the North and the South.

But there's no disputing the fact that the basilica, commonly called the Conewago Chapel, is the nation's oldest Catholic church built of stone, three feet thick at that. Erected by the Jesuits in 1785 and hailed as the "Gem of the Colonial Catholic Churches," the two-and-one-half-story affair is also the first American church dedicated to the Sacred Heart of Jesus.

Big Joe, Biggest Bell

When "Big Joe" — a 35,000-pound bell with a 640-pound clapper — was rung for the first time in 1896 at St. Francis de Sales Church in Cincinnati, Ohio, the earth shook and residents for miles around nearly jumped out of their skins. Reverberations of the E-flat bell shattered windows in the neighborhood and shook mortar loose from the church steeple.

After just one ringing, Big Joe — seven feet tall from rim to crown with a lip nine feet in diameter — was immobilized, never to swing again. Big Joe is no dead ringer, however. A foot hammer now strikes the edge of the country's biggest bell for all to hear.

Doors of Faith

If the Coliseum Church at Our Lady of Martyrs Shrine at Auriesville, near Fultonville, New York, isn't the first coliseum church in the country, it has the most doors: seventy-two of them. Built in 1930–31, the enormous round church recalls the Colosseum in Rome, where many early martyrs met their death. The Coliseum at Auriesville honors three of the eight North American Martyrs: Saints Isaac Jogues, René Goupil, and John Lalande. The three French Jesuits were killed on these grounds, a former Mohawk village, by tomahawk blows in the 1640s. Kateri Tekakwitha, the first Native American saint, was born here in 1656.

Seating 6,500 pilgrims (with standing room for 3,500 more), the Coliseum's seventy-two doors represent the seventy-two disciples sent forth by Jesus (see Lk 10:1). The twelve main aisles and seating sections signify the Twelve Apostles. The crosses carved into the columns imitate Father Jogues's practice of carving crosses into trees during his captivity here. In fact, the shrine grounds are filled with crosses — hundreds of them.

Mega Mary

She stands ninety feet tall and weighs a staggering fifty-one tons. She's the tallest Christian statue in America — the nation's fourth tallest statue overall — and is the fulfillment of a vow. Who is she? *Our Lady of the Rockies* near Butte, Montana.

In 1979, Butte resident Bob O'Bill promised to erect a five-foot statue of Mary in his yard if his wife, Joyce, survived cancer surgery. She did. Within days, however, O'Bill's plans had snowballed into a gigantic Lady atop the Continental Divide, at an elevation of 8,510 feet. Fashioned in six sections of painted white steel, Mega Mary was assumed into Montana heaven by helicopter in December 1985.

Our Lady of the Rockies is more than a mountaintop icon, however. Guided tours take visitors inside the statue (how many statues allow that?), where they can leave a rosary or memento in honor of a loved one. Some visitors claim the Lady's three-foot-wide eyes follow them around the holy mountain. And maybe they do — she's a mother, after all.

Biggest City of the Dead

Calvary Cemetery in Queens, New York, is literally a city of the dead. The largest Catholic cemetery in America, the necropolis encompasses 365 acres. The first burial here took place in 1848; today, more than three million souls await the resurrection. Eternal residents include the likes of Mozart librettist Lorenzo da Ponte, entertainer Dom DeLuise, first Catholic presidential candidate Alfred E. Smith, and Irish lass Annie Moore who, at age seventeen, was the first immigrant processed at Ellis Island when it opened on January 1, 1892.

Never-Too-Late Seminary

Ever wonder how many cookies the average seminarian eats during his four years of priestly formation? At the Pope St. John XXIII National Seminary in Weston, Massachusetts, it's 75,000 homemade cookies! Founded in 1964 by Cardinal Richard J. Cushing of Boston, North America's first seminary for delayed vocations boasts upward of 800 alumni, including three who later became diocesan shepherds: Bishop Paul J. Swain (former lawyer and counsel to the Governor of Wisconsin), Diocese of Sioux Falls, South Dakota; Bishop Robert N. Lynch (former educator), Diocese of St. Petersburg, Florida; and Bishop Roy E. Campbell (former vice president of Bank of America), Auxiliary Bishop of the Archdiocese of Washington.

The never-too-late seminary accepts candidates age thirty and older; the average age of seminarians during the 2024–2025 academic year was fifty-one. Men answering the call come from all walks of life: firefighters, lawyers, an air force intelligence officer, dentist, bankers, a NASA engineer, Anglican converts, and widowers with grandchildren. While the oldest seminarian here was seventy-one years old when ordained, he was a "youngster" compared to an even later vocation — William Murphy.

After helping to build a number of Catholic churches in North Carolina, Murphy, a septuagenarian, decided to become a priest and entered Saint Meinrad Seminary at St. Meinrad, Indiana. Younger seminarians — young enough to be his grandsons — teased their senior classmate that he was taking a crash course in extreme unction! Murphy was ordained in 1972, at age eighty. He served St. Margaret of Scotland Catholic Church in Maggie Valley, North Carolina — a church he had built in the late 1960s — until his death in 1991, at age ninety-nine.

Longest Prayer

How long is the country's longest-running prayer? Nearly 142 years! From August 1, 1878, through February 25, 2020, at least two people kept vigil in shifts around the clock in Maria Angelorum Chapel at the Franciscan Sisters of Perpetual Adoration in La Crosse, Wisconsin. That's over 1.2 million hours of nonstop prayer! Today, prayer rises like incense before the Blessed Sacrament from 6 a.m. to 10 p.m. Keeping watch over the gorgeous Romanesque-style chapel is a choir of all-seeing cherubim: Their stained glass feathers have eyes.

Possibly surpassing the La Crosse record one day is the National Shrine of St. Maximilian Kolbe at Marytown in Libertyville, Illinois. In 1928, the Benedictine Sisters of Perpetual Adoration of Clyde, Missouri, instituted 24/7 prayer here in Our Lady of the Blessed Sacrament Chapel. Fifty years later, the Conventual Franciscans from Kenosha, Wisconsin, bought the regal chapel, where perpetual adoration continues to this day. The radiant stained glass windows include ninety-nine Eucharistic symbols; incredibly, not one symbol is duplicated.

Biggest Monstrance(s)

When the sanctuary curtains parted on May 31, 2008, at St. Stanislaus Kostka Church in Chicago and revealed a nine-foot-by-nine-foot monstrance, jaws dropped. *Our Lady of the Sign, Ark of Mercy* is unlike any monstrance, anywhere. Carved of linden wood by Polish sculptor Stefan Niedorezo, the polychrome monstrance is America's biggest. The iconic vessel portrays the Blessed Mother atop a gold-leafed ark flanked by two golden angels, their gigantic wings sheltering her. Encased in Our Lady's center is a six-inch luna that holds the sacred Host, surrounded by a crown of thorns. The monstrance honors Mary as the Ark of the Covenant.

\+ + + + +

You can't help but fall to your knees before the country's biggest traditionally styled monstrance, venerated at the Shrine of the Most Blessed Sacrament at Our Lady of the Angels Monastery in Hanceville, Alabama. Resembling a golden sunburst, the resplendent, nearly eight-foot-tall monstrance stands high above the altar, the Eucharist enthroned at the center of a jeweled cross. Four golden angels offer praise and honor to the Lord of hosts.

Church You Can't Visit

The Church of St. Dismas, the Good Thief, at Dannemora, New York, has a select congregation: prisoners. Located at Clinton Correctional Facility, a maximum security prison, St. Dismas is the nation's first freestanding church built inside prison walls. Father Ambrose Hyland, prison chaplain, and inmates began building the 8,000-square-foot, neo-Gothic stone structure in 1939. Hyland thought the convicts — and God himself — deserved a better chapel than a decrepit auditorium under the mess hall.

To decorate the church, Hyland recruited talented prisoners and had outside artisans come in to train them. A convicted forger crafted the Stations of the Cross stained glass windows, using inmates as models. Even the child in the Eighth Station has an inmate's face. A sculpture of Saint Dismas captures the agony of his crucifixion alongside Christ on Good Friday. When the convict posing as the Good Thief — standing on a bucket, his arms bound to a cross — didn't show the requisite pain needed by the inmate-artist to sculpt the face, the bucket was kicked from under his feet.

Extreme Trivia QUESTION 4

Erected in 1841, this limestone cathedral is heralded for its Greek Revival design and striking single spire, which soars 224 feet above street level. It's also been called the "bishop factory." Name the cathedral and the "bishop maker."

Come Fly with Mary

There's only one way to fly: with the Blessed Mother. That's what then-Archbishop Richard J. Cushing thought in 1952 when he dedicated Our Lady of the Airways Chapel — the nation's first airport chapel — at what is now Boston Logan International Airport in Boston, Massachusetts.

Called "one of the most unusual chapels in the world," the oratory was built as a workers' chapel, where airport employees and business travelers could attend Mass and receive the sacraments. The chapel featured a circular sanctuary with a circular communion rail and was adorned with a statue of *Our Lady of the Airways*, three small planes encircling her feet. When the chapel was later moved to another site within the airport, Our Lady and her planes went too.

The Man on the Cross

The "Old Rugged Cross" ascends to record heights at the Cross in the Woods Catholic Shrine at Indian River, located in the northern Michigan town of Indian River. Hanging on the fifty-five-foot-tall cross — made from a single redwood tree — the bronze corpus of Christ weighs seven tons and measures twenty-eight feet from head to toe. His outstretched arms span twenty-one feet. Christ was "nailed to the cross" in 1959 with thirteen bolts thirty inches long and two inches thick.

When renowned Michigan sculptor Marshall Fredericks created *The Man on the Cross*, he wanted the figure to exude a sense of peace. Rather than portraying Christ with a crown of thorns and a wound in his side, the sculptor presents Christ at the moment he commends his spirit to the Father. The breathtaking scene stands on an earthen knoll fifteen feet high, making it the tallest crucifix in the country.

First Credit Union

You can "bank" on St. Mary's Bank — the nation's first credit union — in Manchester, New Hampshire. In 1908, Monsignor Pierre Hevey, pastor of Manchester's Ste. Marie Church, founded the enterprise for French Canadian mill workers denied savings and borrowing privileges at local banks. As it turned out, St. Mary's Bank was a stellar financial institution. When thousands of banks nationwide failed during the Great Depression, St. Mary's remained open — even during President Franklin D. Roosevelt's "Bank Holiday" of 1933.

The original bank, which was located in the home of Joseph Boivin, an attorney and the credit union's first president, now houses America's Credit Union Museum.

Oldest Lady Statue

A true lady never reveals her age, and neither does *La Conquistadora*. The country's oldest Marian statue, *La Conquistadora* is at least 400 years old and reigns from the nation's oldest extant Marian shrine: a 1714 adobe chapel at the Cathedral Basilica of St. Francis of Assisi in Santa Fe, New Mexico. It's believed the twenty-eight-inch wooden Madonna was carved in Spain and brought to New Mexico by Franciscan friar Alonso de Benavides in 1625.

But the title *La Conquistadora* (who can escape her striking blue eyes?) has nothing to do with conquering others. Rather, she "conquers" hearts through her love and that of her divine Son. A hole in the statue's core has historians baffled. Was she mounted on a standard and carried in processions in Old Spain? In battles? *¿Quién sabe?*

In another curious nugget, *La Conquistadora* may be the only statue with a body double. *La Peregrina* (The Pilgrim) is used as a stand-in when *La Conquistadora* makes appearances at fiestas, processions, and other public functions.

Wee Churches

The competition for America's smallest Catholic church is gigantic. Billed as the "World's Smallest Catholic Church," St. Martin's near Warrenton, Texas, seats twenty. The church wasn't always so bite-size, though. When built in 1888, the church measured thirty-six by sixty-eight feet. Who shrank St. Martin's? In 1915, the parish wanted a school, so the church was dismantled for its lumber. The leftover boards were used to build the wee roadside attraction.

+ + + + +

A little bit o' heaven, Our Lady of the Pines Church at Silver Lake (near Thomas), West Virginia, "spans" twelve by twenty-four feet. Peter L. Milkint, a Lithuanian immigrant, and his wife, Elizabeth, erected the quaint sandstone church in 1958 in memory of their parents. The six wooden pews fit two people each. Right next door is an even tinier building: a mail drop for church postcards.

+ + + + +

Built in 1885 to fulfill a mother's pledge if her son returned home from war, St. Anthony of Padua Chapel near Festina, Iowa, seats a grand total of eight. What's more, the charming fourteen-by-twenty-foot stone structure with belfry was built by distant relatives of Saint Anthony himself. This "Smallest Church in the World" is located in the Smallest Church Park.

+ + + + +

Perhaps the teeniest church of all is St. Joseph's Chapel near tiny Warsaw, North Dakota. Built in 1907 by eight Polish pioneers

(four of them named Joe) who settled along the Red River of the North, the white frame chapel with three steeples is so teeny that only a priest and two altar boys can squeeze inside — if everyone holds their breath.

Wholly Relics

Father Suitbert G. Mollinger had a unique hobby: collecting relics of saints. By the time the Belgian immigrant breathed his last in 1892, he had amassed some 5,000 of them — the world's largest collection of relics outside the Vatican. The relics are housed in over 800 reliquaries, floor to ceiling, at Saint Anthony Chapel in Pittsburgh, Pennsylvania. Romanesque in design, the ornate, hilltop chapel cost the priest a pretty penny to build: $300,000 of his family inheritance ($9 million today).

Relics include a thorn from the Crown of Thorns, a fragment of the Blessed Mother's veil, bones from all twelve of Jesus' apostles, a golden sarcophagus with the full skeleton of Saint Demetrius, skulls of the martyred companions of Saint Ursula, and a tooth of the wonderworker St. Anthony of Padua.

Largest Artistic Glass Window

Did dinosaurs frolic in the Garden of Eden? They do in the world's largest artistic glass installation at Resurrection Cemetery Mausoleum, an eye-popping Greek-inspired temple at Justice, Illinois. Covering 22,381 square feet, the four-story-tall window of faceted glass wraps around the entire building and tells in dramatic reds, greens, oranges, and blues the story of time. The 2,448 panels include Pharoah cracking a whip, a lion's fangs dripping with Christian blood, and Jesus standing on a ship's prow. Airplanes, a satellite dish, and an atomic mushroom cloud bring the scenes current to 1969, when the architectural landmark went up.

Biggest Rosary

For big prayer needs, pray the country's biggest rosary at Our Lady of Fatima Shrine in Holliston, Massachusetts. It measures some 1,000 feet long and weighs many hundreds of tons! The granite Hail Mary "beads" — joined by chain from a ship's anchor — are waist high, and the Our Father beads are reputedly twice as big. The Hail Mary beads each bear plaques with the Hail Mary prayer inscribed in a different language — from Old Arabic to Inuit to Tamil.

As big as the Holliston rosary is, it's small compared to the Rosary of Lebanon, located near Deir El Ahmar in northern Lebanon. The beads of this nearly 2,000-foot-long rosary are big enough for pilgrims to walk through.

One Man's Cathedral

Thomas J. O'Neill (1849–1919) was a merchant with a "great pearl": His munificence built the Cathedral of Mary Our Queen in Baltimore, Maryland — the nation's only cathedral financed by just one person. Yet the great pearl almost didn't happen. On February 7, 1904, the Great Baltimore Fire was roaring toward O'Neill's international dry goods store. The Irish immigrant raced to a nearby Carmelite monastery and begged prayers to save his store and the livelihoods of 500 employees. Just as the flames began licking the store's south wall, the winds abruptly shifted.

In gratitude for the miraculous save, O'Neill bequeathed $5 million (worth $91 million today) for a new cathedral in Baltimore. The Great Depression and the Second World War delayed building plans, and by the time the Archdiocese of Baltimore was ready to begin construction in the mid-1950s, O'Neill's bequest, through prudent investing, had nearly doubled.

Designed in modified Gothic style with art deco accents, the cathedral is a behemoth. The limestone structure is 373 feet long (forty-one feet longer than St. Patrick's Cathedral in New York City) and 163 feet high. The interior boasts over 385 sculptures and 398 panels of stained glass. In a side chapel, O'Neill, a daily Mass goer, appears in stained glass with a missal and his will in hand.

Mary's First Garden

To Jesus through Mary — and her flowers at Mary Garden in Woods Hole, a Cape Cod village in Massachusetts. Proclaimed the country's first public garden dedicated to Mary, the waterside retreat began in 1932 with Frances Crane Lillie. A Catholic convert, Lillie wanted to remind the local oceanographic community that there are more mysteries in life than science.

Each of the flowers in Mary Garden — from Lady's Slippers to Assumption Lilies to Mary's Prayers (tulips) — recall an event in Mary's life or one of her virtues. The Staff of Saint Joseph (hollyhocks) represents Joseph, Mary's husband. St. Joseph Chapel is located opposite the garden. Lillie also built the neighboring Angelus Bell Tower. The two bells are named for famed Catholic scientists Gregor Mendel and Louis Pasteur.

Sister, Oh Sister!

Get in the "habit" at the Doll Museum at Cross in the Woods Catholic Shrine of Indian River, located at Indian River, Michigan — the nation's largest collection of nun dolls. As a young girl, Sally Rogalski was fascinated with nuns and began dressing dolls in authentic reproductions of habits — from black to blue and even pink — worn by religious sisters before Vatican II. Mother Seton's Sisters of Charity dolls wear the widow's dress of her era, and Mother Teresa's Missionaries of Charity dolls are clad in a white sari with blue stripes. You can't miss the "flying nuns": The Daughters of Charity dolls wear white peasant headgear that resembles wings.

Boasting over 525 dolls that represent nearly 220 religious orders worldwide, the doll collection also displays life-size mannequins of both women religious and male clergy, including a mitered bishop. And no, Father Mannequin doesn't hear confessions.

Oldest Bishop

According to the *Guinness Book of World Records*, the oldest bishop in America was Archbishop Edward D. Howard of Portland, Oregon. Born on November 5, 1877, he died at age 105 on January 2, 1983. His older twin brother, however, lived just nine months. It's estimated that Howard celebrated at least 27,800

Masses — one Mass daily during his seventy-six-plus years as a priest. He was a prelate for over fifty-eight years.

When Howard wanted an archdiocesan high school for boys in Portland, he didn't let anything stop him, not even a cemetery. He moved the dead (not that they objected) across town. Central Catholic High School opened its doors in 1939. The school, now coed, is still in operation today.

Extreme Trivia
QUESTION 5

"We offer you: no salary, no recompense, no holidays, no pensions. But, much hard work, a poor dwelling, few consolations, many disappointments, frequent sickness, a violent or lonely death, an unknown grave." This advertisement appeared in a newspaper in France. Who was this ad recruiting?

Section Two

INCREDIBLE CHURCHES AND CHURCH ART

What color are God's eyes? Where can you pay your respects to the Sorrowful Mother on Good Friday? Where can you sit in "double-jointed" pews? Or experience the thrill of bilocating? How many miles to Wall Drug (Chapel)? Which Last Supper painting is so hot it could burn your tongue? Why is the loneliest statue in America so lonely? You'll find the answers to these questions and much more in this section dedicated to America's Incredible Catholic Churches and Church Art. You won't believe your eyes — or ears.

Our Lady and the Locusts

When a plague of Rocky Mountain locusts invaded Cold Spring, Minnesota, in 1876, the "flying demons" ate everything but the mortgages. The locusts (or grasshoppers as the settlers called them) devoured crops and gardens to the quick, stripped the trees bare, and even attacked the livestock. Spring planting in 1877 looked dismal: Millions of grasshopper eggs were ready to hatch. Homesteaders were terrified. How would they survive? What would they do for food?

Inspired by Father Leo Winter, OSB, pastor, the German-speaking settlers appealed to *Maria Hilf* (German for "Mary, Help!") and vowed to build her a chapel to avert the plague. As soon as construction began on July 16 — feast of Our Lady of Mount Carmel — the hoppers took wing. Maria Hilf not only drove out the flying demons, but she annihilated the insect. The Rocky Mountain locust is now believed to be extinct.

Constructed of granite in 1951, Assumption Chapel (locally called the Grasshopper Chapel) occupies the old chapel site. A locust repellant of sorts, a granite tympanum over the front doors depicts Mary's Assumption into heaven, two hoppers under her feet.

Blood of a Saint

Venerable Nelson Baker (1842–1936) lived by miracles — miracles wrought by Our Lady of Victory. In 1921, when the seventy-nine-year-old priest began erecting a grand temple for "his Lady" at Lackawanna, New York, he didn't have a dime. When OLV National Shrine and Basilica was completed five years later, at an estimated cost of $3.2 million, he didn't owe a nickel!

Is Our Lady returning the favor with the spectacle of Baker's blood? In 1999, his remains were transferred from nearby Holy Cross Cemetery to the basilica. When his body was disinterred, a jar of Baker's blood was found inside a small concrete vault on top of his coffin. To everyone's astonishment, the blood hadn't dried — it was still liquid. Not even Januarius, the famous Italian saint, can lay claim to that. His dried blood, contained in a special reliquary, only liquefies on designated days each year.

Hands of Christ

When renowned artist George C. Tooker (1920–2011) was asked to paint the Stations of the Cross for St. Francis of Assisi Church in Windsor, Vermont, newly built in 1980, the Catholic convert said he wasn't worthy to paint the body of Our Lord. Instead, Tooker used Christ's hands as the narrative expression. Deciphering Christ's hands, however, takes contemplation. When Christ meets his Sorrowful Mother in the Fourth Station, a masculine hand appears with a softer, feminine hand. In the Eleventh Station, a nail-pierced hand symbolizes Christ's crucifixion, and a lifeless hand in the Twelfth Station, his death.

Take That, Devil!

The devil doesn't stand a chance at St. Benedict's Painted Church, located at Captain Cook on the Big Island of Hawaii. Using house paint, Father John Berchmans Velghe, SS.CC, adorned the wooden interior, walls to vaulted ceiling, in religious folk art. He also left specific instructions for the devil: "Drink your own poison!" Written in Hawaiian on the painted red pillars — made from trunks of coconut palm trees — is the St. Benedict medal's prayer of exorcism.

While 125 years have passed since Velghe decorated the church, St. Benedict's is still giving the devil his due. When tourists visit the Painted Church, as it's called, they want to know what the red pillars say. Thus, the exorcism prayer gets recited again and again — and the devil gets booted out again and again.

Mystical Shroud

The Shroud of Turin replica at the Dominican Monastery of Our Lady of the Rosary in Summit, New Jersey, is more than a true copy of the Holy Shroud — it's a 400-year-old sacred mystery. According to authenticated records, the Shroud replica was commissioned in 1624 by Maria Maddalena of Austria, Grand Duchess of Tuscany, wife of Cosimo de' Medici. To give the replica more spiritual import, it was placed for a time on the original Shroud of Turin, believed to be the burial cloth of Jesus.

When the replica was removed, a damp blood stain appeared on the replica that matched a stain from Jesus' side on the original, as though Jesus himself had bled onto the replica. The Grand Duchess gave the Shroud copy to the Dominican nuns of St. Catherine's Monastery in Rome. Three centuries later, in 1924, St. Catherine's nuns gifted the replica to the New Jersey nuns in thanksgiving for their abundant help in the wake of World War I. In 1987, scientists from STURP (Shroud of Turin Research Project) confirmed the stain on the replica was indeed human blood and the same blood type as that found on the Holy Shroud itself.

"Calamity St. Rose"

The gigantic gauge painted on the exterior brick wall of St. Rose of Lima Catholic Church in Cincinnati, Ohio, isn't a fundraising gimmick. It's a flood gauge! The gauge, overlooking the Ohio River, marks fifteen floods: 1884, 1913, 1918, 1930, 1933, 1937, 1945, 1948, 1963, 1964, 1966, 1978, 1979, 1982, and 1997. The highest flood was the eighty-foot flood of 1937 (water enters the church basement at the fifty-seven-foot mark). There have been so many floods at the German-built church that St. Rose on the Ohio earned the moniker "St. Rose in the Ohio."

Floods haven't been the only disasters at "Calamity St. Rose." On January 31, 1894, an altar boy lighting candles on the high altar for a wedding accidentally set the church on fire. The bridal couple got married at a nearby church and came back to watch the blaze. Their wedding day had gone up in smoke. The gorgeous Romanesque church, rebuilt in July 1894, may be the only American church with a thimble, a pin cushion, and two needles (one with thread) painted on its apse ceiling. Church patron St. Rose of Lima earned her living by sewing.

Exalted Cathedral

Everything about St. Patrick's Cathedral in New York City is massive. Built between 1858 and 1879, St. Patrick's is hailed as the largest neo-Gothic Catholic cathedral in the nation. The interior is 380 feet long, while the 330-foot-tall twin spires are practically knocking at heaven's doors. The bronze doors on Fifth Avenue weigh over 9,000 pounds each, and the nineteen bells are each named for a different saint. It's said if you listen carefully enough, you can hear the nineteen names echoing in the tintinnabulation of the bells.

When Archbishop John J. Hughes began building the new cathedral in 1858 to replace St. Patrick's Old Cathedral (now a basilica), people scoffed and called it "Hughes's Folly." What sense did it make to build such a vast cathedral in the boonies? Today, St. Patrick's stands smack dab in the heart of New York City and is among the city's top tourist attractions.

Extreme Trivia
QUESTION 6

How many islands make up the Apostle Islands in Lake Superior, off the Bayfield Peninsula in northwestern Wisconsin?

Swastika Church

Built in 1929 on the eve of the Great Depression, St. Mary's Catholic Church in Umbarger, Texas, was white as a barn inside.

White walls. White windows. White Stations of the Cross. Everything was white except for the wooden altars and statues. One day in 1945, the pastor decided to "color" the Panhandle church: He recruited Italian POW-artists incarcerated at nearby Camp Hereford. The POWs painted the three Marian images in the apse, carved the Last Supper scene for the altar front, decorated the nave with religious symbols, polychromed the Stations, installed the stained glass windows, and more.

Some decades later, one of the Italian artists returned to St. Mary's for a visit. During his stay, the artist revealed swastikas hidden in two murals behind the statues of Jesus and Mary. Parishioners were shocked! In all those years, nobody had noticed. The swastikas — a type of a cross — were cleverly disguised as a backdrop in the two murals that are filled with gold crosses. The gold crosses catch the eye but not the thinner, interlocking swastikas behind them.

Chapels on Steel Wheels

Wherever the railroad went, the Church was sure to follow — with railroad chapel cars. Inspired by Episcopal and American Baptist chapel cars that brought the Gospel to people living off the beaten track, Father Francis Clement Kelly, founder of the Catholic Church Extension Society (now Catholic Extension) in 1905, rolled out three Catholic chapel cars.

A converted 1886 Wagner car, the wooden *St. Anthony* — seventy-two-feet long with living quarters for the priest and a chapel seating fifty — hit the rails in 1907 and served chiefly in the Pacific Northwest. When the *St. Anthony* rolled into a town, Mass was offered and baptisms and marriages performed. Tough hombres who wouldn't darken the doors of any church were lured like a magnet to the novelty chapel car.

Dedicated in 1912, the eighty-four-foot *St. Peter* was built of steel. Of Gothic design, the interior was trimmed in rich mahog-

any and sat seventy. The "Steel Apostle" headed West to join the *St. Anthony*. Evangelizing by rail wasn't heaven on earth, however. In one Oregon town, lore has it, a man ordered the chapel car priest to take off his shoes and socks. He wanted to see if the priest had cloven feet, a sure sign of the devil.

The *St. Paul* measured eighty-six feet long and featured observation decks on both ends and chapel space for seventy-five. Christened in 1915, the steel ark ministered in the South and Southeast. In 1924, when the *St. Paul* was parked on a siding in Plymouth, North Carolina, chapel missionary Father Stephen Sweeney, CP, received a "welcome note" from the Ku Klux Klan: Get out of town! Sweeney placed his confidence in the Blessed Sacrament aboard the chapel car. "Our friends of the Invisible Empire did not so much as burn a cross," he later reported.

As automobiles became more affordable and people could travel longer distances to church, the rolling chapels fell out of use. Many hundreds of parishes were formed and churches built as a result of the chapel car visits. And that is how frontier America was really won — by missionaries on iron horses.

Only two chapel cars, both sent forth by the American Baptist Publication Society, exist today for public viewing. While not Catholic, they offer a glimpse into the fascinating era of chapel cars. *Chapel Car Grace* is located at Green Lake Conference Center in Green Lake, Wisconsin, and *Chapel Car Emmanuel* is part of Historic Prairie Village at Madison, South Dakota.

Fish Church

If ever there was a whale of a church, it's St. Francis Xavier Catholic Church in Kansas City, Missouri. The oval-shaped church with tail-like entrance mimics a giant fish, an ancient symbol of Christ. Inside, the tall blue windows impart the feeling of being at sea with other fish — in this case, one's fellow parishioners. And no, Jonah isn't here. Known as "Kansas City's Jesuit Parish," the hilltop concrete church was dedicated in 1950.

Raising a Church

You've heard of barn raisings, but a church raising? It happened in 1889 at St. Ambrose Church in Richmond, Maine. Townsfolk — Catholic and Protestant — came together like an Amish barn raising to put up the frame church. The dedication Mass on December 15, 1889, was also a community affair: More Protestants filled the pews than Catholics!

Artist Who?

Life has its lighter side. In 1945, an artist arrived at Assumption of the Blessed Virgin Mary Catholic Church in Florence, Arizona, to paint the pastel backdrop for a gorgeous statue of Mary's Assumption. High above the main altar, the artist executed dreamy clouds and cherubim that seem to be transporting the blue-robed statue of Mary into heaven. The artist? An inmate at a nearby prison with the unlikely name of Monet.

Loneliest Statue

The statue of Christ the King on Alaska's King Island — some eighty-five miles from Nome on the mainland — is the loneliest statue in America. Jutting out of the Bering Sea, the small, craggy island was once the winter home of the Inupiat, traditionally walrus hunters and ivory carvers. In 1929, Father Bellarmine Lafortune, SJ, built a frame church atop a steep slope covered with houses on stilts and dedicated the island mission to Christ the King.

When the statue arrived on the island in 1937, Inupiat men and boys hauled the 900-pound bronze king up to his throne on a 700-foot cliff above the village. The King Islanders dedicated themselves to the King of kings and for over two decades made pilgrimages to the statue to pray. Murre birds came too and laid eggs at his feet. The Bureau of Indian Affairs closed the islet school in 1959, and the 200 or so King Islanders moved to the mainland. Christ the King still reigns over their ancestral home, a lonely figure on a lonely island.

"Potato Chip" Church

No one attends Mass just once at St. Charles Catholic Church in Spokane, Washington. Why? Because the wavy roof — a hyperbolic paraboloid of three-inch-thick concrete — looks like a potato chip. And who eats just one chip? The stained glass "sky windows" add to the allure. Located just below the roofline, the windows give the illusion that the wavy roof is floating over the nave. When completed in 1961, the architecturally historic church was touted as the largest building of its kind in the world.

Pillars of the Church

Who's holding up the church? In Sisters, Oregon, a one-of-a-kind cloister of carved saints. Thirty-four caryatids — or load-bearing statues — support the roof of St. Edward the Mar-

tyr Catholic Church. Sculpted by J. Chester Armstrong, the pine log statues are more than carved saints with wooden whiskers, veils, and halos. Each larger-than-life statue also holds a model of its namesake church in the Diocese of Baker.

A bird perched atop his tonsured head and a squirrel on his shoulder, the caryatid of St. Francis of Assisi holds a replica of St. Francis Church in Bend. Little boy Jesus clings to his mama, as little children do, in the Holy Family pillar dedicated to Holy Family Church in Burns. St. Kateri Tekakwitha clutches a basket of corn and a turtle in one hand, a replica of her Warm Springs church in the other.

Sixteen of the thirty-four caryatids stand guard inside the church, while the other eighteen pillars, visible through the floor-to-ceiling glass wall, hold up the roof overlooking St. Winefride's Garden. The cloistered garden features a waterfall with meandering stream and stained glass Stations of the Risen Christ.

Everywhere you look, saints are holding up St. Edward the Martyr Catholic Church — in more ways than one.

Wedding Stairs

Get down on your knees if you want to ascend the Holy Stairs inside St. Patrick Church at Pittsburgh and say a prayer on each step. The twenty-eight white marble steps imitate the Scala Sancta in Rome and lead to the main altar and worship space on the second floor. Only a bride and her father are allowed to walk up the stairs — thought to be the only indoor Holy Stairs in the United States — and then the bride and her new groom on the way down.

Sweetest Grotto

The Lourdes Grotto at St. Michael the Archangel Church in Convent, Louisiana, is the sweetest grotto ever. Tucked behind the altar, the grotto — constructed eighteen years after Our Lady appeared in 1858 to St. Bernadette Soubirous at Lourdes, France — also pays homage to the local sugarcane industry. The grotto "stones" were made of bagasse, the pulpy residue left after the juice from sugarcane has been extracted. The dome was fashioned from an overturned sugar kettle. The "Sweetest Grotto" is one of the premier Lourdes shrines in the country.

Condolences to Mary

There is no Good Friday ritual like the Procession and Pésame at Ysleta Mission in El Paso, Texas. The *Santo Entierro* — a three-centuries-old wooden statue of Christ Interred (the 1722 date is stamped on his feet) — is carried in procession on a bier around the mission. The life-size statue is then brought back into the historic adobe church. As mourners file past the *Santo Entierro,* they stop to offer *pésame* (condolences) to a statue of the Sorrowful Mother. Her sorrow becomes their sorrow, and many begin to weep in her presence.

Historically called La Misión de Corpus Christi de San Antonio de la Ysleta del Sur (Mission of the Body of Christ of Saint Anthony of Ysleta of the South), Ysleta Mission was founded c. 1682 for Christianized Indians who had fled New Mexico during the Pueblo Revolt of 1680. Nearly 350 years old, Ysleta Mission is the oldest continuously operating parish in Texas.

God's Eye

What color is God's all-seeing eye? Would you believe blue? At St. James Church, built in 1912 in the Highlands area of Louisville, Kentucky, an enormous blue eye of glass tile in the eighty-foot dome ceiling keeps squirming kids (and adults, mind you) in line. The white of the eye is so white that it makes the eye appear like a giant telescope zooming in on souls seated below. The human-looking eye — with upper and lower eyelids even — is rumored to be one of few such eyeballs in the world.

Hail Mary!

Where can you find the Blessed Mother? In paintings and statues everywhere! She also appears in some out-of-the-ordinary images across our land.

At Carmel of Mary Monastery near Wahpeton, North Dakota, a snow-white statue of Our Lady of the Prairies stands in an outdoor shrine, holding a real sheaf of wheat. Not only do birds make frequent pilgrimages to the shrine to dine on the wheat, but it's said there hasn't been a bad wheat crop in the region since the barefoot Lady arrived in 1957.

\+ + + + +

Our Lady attends every Mass, every wedding, every prayer service at St. Mary's Church in Boise, Idaho. In fact, she's seated in a front-row pew. Sculpted by local artist John Taye, the life-size bronze statue is a popular photo op: Everyone wants their photo taken with Mama Mary! Even the littlest tykes know this Lady is special and crawl up into her lap for a holy snuggle.

\+ + + + +

The Blessed Mother was a real mother with real chores to do. In a stained glass window depicting the Holy Family at the Cathedral of St. Paul in Birmingham, Alabama, the Lady of the House engages in the domestic art of spinning wool. Did the boy Jesus need a new tunic? He was growing up so fast, as children do. Joseph is there, too, with his carpentry tools.

\+ + + + +

At Immaculate Heart of Mary Church in Pittsburgh, Pennsylvania, a statue of Mary keeps the founding families close to her heart: She wears a locket with their names. The opulent Polish church was built on a hill so that worshippers would feel closer to God.

Where East Meets West

Old St. Patrick's Church, in the West Loop of Chicago, has all the luck of the Irish. Nearly 175 years old, the cream-colored brick church escaped the Great Chicago Fire of 1871, by a mere two blocks. In 1950, it escaped the demolition ball. But St. Pat's couldn't escape the urban flight. When Father John J. Wall be-

came pastor in 1983, he counted the registered parishioners on four fingers. Luckily for Old St. Pat's, Wall launched a "church in the marketplace" plan to attract young adults and working professionals and threw the first "World's Largest Block Party" in 1985. Within four years, the registered households had zoomed to over 1,000 — a phenomenal increase of nearly 25,000 percent!

Then again, Old St. Pat's isn't your typical church: It's where East meets West. The pointed spire of the Romanesque landmark represents the Roman Catholic or Western rite of the Church, and the onion-domed tower the Byzantine or Eastern rite. Together, they symbolically encompass all of Catholic Christendom. Even Saint Patrick would be impressed.

Mass in Glass

How many American Catholic churches have stained glass designed by a renowned book illustrator? Only one: St. Vincent de Paul Church in Bayonne, New Jersey. A book illustrator for Hans Christian Andersen and Edgar Allen Poe, Harry Clarke illuminated his Mass in Glass with animated faces and mesmerizing eyes that draw people into the Masses. When people attend Mass at St. Vincent's, they're also in the presence of eleven stained glass Masses being offered at once.

The stained glass wonders depict bishops and priests celebrating Masses for special intentions, including the Mass of Ordination, Mass of the Holy Angels, Mass of the Holy Spirit, Nuptial Mass, and Mass of First Communion. Based in Dublin, Ireland, Clarke (1889–1931) portrayed himself as a poor soul being prayed for in the Mass of the Holy Souls window.

Saddest Statue

Standing outside St. Joseph's Old Cathedral in Oklahoma City, Oklahoma, is the saddest statue in the United States. Titled *And Jesus Wept*, a nine-foot, white-marble sculpture of Christ — head bowed and face covered with one hand — weeps over the loss of life during the April 19, 1995, bombing of the nearby Alfred P. Murrah Federal Building. A black granite wall with 168 niches represents the 168 lives lost in the horrific blast.

St. Joseph's Old Cathedral was heavily damaged in the explosion, but amazingly the blast did not extinguish the tabernacle light, nor did the crucifix with a life-size corpus of Jesus suffer mutilation from the flying debris and shattered glass.

Mystery Carpenter

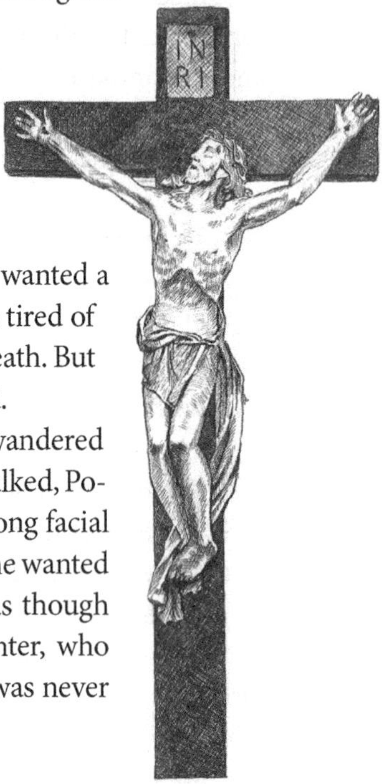

When Moravian immigrant Albin Polasek (1879–1965) was sculpting the seven-foot bronze corpus that hangs on a thirteen-foot-tall cross at Saint Cecilia Cathedral in Omaha, Nebraska, he wanted a unique expression for Christ's face. He was tired of the usual pose — Jesus' head slumped in death. But he was stuck in limbo as to how to proceed.

One day, tradition holds, a stranger wandered in asking for work as a carpenter. As they talked, Polasek became fascinated with the man's strong facial features. Suddenly, the sculptor knew how he wanted to create Christ's face: turned to heaven, as though saying, "Father, forgive them." The carpenter, who was to return the next day to begin work, was never seen again.

Bilocate at This Church

Experience the thrill of bilocating at St. Peter Catholic Church in Memphis, Tennessee, and stand in two churches at once. The first church was erected in 1842. When the parish outgrew that building, the present Norman Gothic fortress was erected up and around the old church, a common practice back in the day.

When the new St. Peter's was ready for roofing, the old building was taken down and carried out the front doors.

Tended by Dominican friars since 1846, the church is touted for its fabulous stained glass windows, including a "look-alike" window. A memorial to parishioners who served in World War I, the window portrays a soldier and a sailor, on bended knee, surrounded by Dominican saints. Lore has it the faces of the saints bear an uncanny resemblance to the pastor who ordered the window. Apparently, the pastor thought he was a saint in the making.

Church of the Holy Haircut

St. Ann Church in Cleveland Heights, Ohio, began with a haircut. In 1925, Father John Mary Powers, pastor, went downtown to see a barber. He walked by a bank that had recently failed. Since he needed a desk, he dropped in. Powers not only bought a used desk but the bank's pillars, chandeliers, a huge clock, and even the bronze and brass doors, some say. Then, the bargain hunter purchased used marble from the Ritz Carlton Hotel in New York City, two balconies from a Hanna family mansion, and later an altar from an old seminary. Beautiful St. Ann Church is the brilliant merger of a bank, a hotel, a mansion, and a seminary. It pays to get a haircut.

Double-Jointed Pews

Built in a pioneer town too small to support two churches, the Little Church at Keystone, Nebraska, is an interfaith marvel. Seating seventy, the 1908 wooden chapel measures just eighteen by forty feet and features two apses: a Protestant altar on one end and a Catholic altar and confessional at the other end. Hinges on pew ends allowed worshippers to flip the pew-backs to face the altar of their faith. The only door to the church was aptly positioned between the two altars.

The last Mass offered here was in 1929 and the last Protestant service two decades later. Made famous by *Ripley's Believe It or Not*, the Little Church at Keystone still stands — in a little town that's still too small for two churches.

Extreme Trivia
QUESTION 7

On September 11, 1987, Pope St. John Paul II, successor of St. Peter the Apostle, held an audience at this American church named Saint Peter's. Elevated to a basilica in 2018, the church is also known for its historic cemetery, including one graveyard resident who lived in three centuries. Where is this basilica?

Depression Grotto

Many shrines are erected to fulfill a vow after prayers have already been answered, but not the Grotto of St. Boniface near Grenora, North Dakota. It was built in 1931 as a plea to God for help. It was the worst of times. The northern plains had been hit hard by the Great Depression and the Dirty Thirties. Gigantic clouds of dirt — miles long and thousands of feet high — rolled across the open expanse, creating drifts just like snow. Dirt drifts covered fences and vehicles. Livestock died of "dust pneumonia." Nothing grew, except fear.

Looking to heaven for relief, the farming community gathered fieldstones and constructed an immense curved grotto — wider than it is tall — to the Blessed Mother at St. Boniface Cemetery in Good Luck Township. A statue of Mary and an altar were placed deep inside the man-made cave, safe from the elements. Here, weary souls prayed and thanked God for his providence, even in the worst of times.

Underground Mystery

During renovations in 2019 at the Basilica of St. Mary of the Immaculate Conception in downtown Norfolk, Virginia, two mystery tunnels were discovered. Were the brick tunnels — about three feet by four feet — part of the Underground Railroad, an escape route for slaves to the free North? A port city, Norfolk was a hub on the clandestine railroad.

There's no speculation about the basilica's dramatic past, however. The original church was built in 1842 and called St. Patrick's. A decade later, Father Matthew O'Keefe arrived as pastor of the mixed-race parish and drew the ire of the nativist Know-Nothings. They wanted the integrated Masses stopped. O'Keefe received so many threats against him and the church that police protection was needed. It wasn't enough. On December 8, 1856, the church burned down, allegedly set on fire by the Know-Nothings.

The present church, of antebellum French Gothic design, was dedicated in 1858 to St. Mary of the Immaculate Conception. The new name was an apt choice: St. Patrick's had gone up in smoke on her feast day. Though non-white Catholics were once relegated to pews in the choir loft, St. Mary's is a predominantly Black congregation today. It is the only African American basilica in the nation.

"Tabasco" Last Supper

When Father Bryce Sibley commissioned Christie Hebert Hollier in the early 2000s to paint a medallion of the Last Supper for St. Joseph Catholic Church in Parks, Louisiana, he wanted to spice it up. He asked the artist to include a bottle of Tabasco hot sauce! Sitting on the table, before Jesus and four of his disciples, are platters of food and the iconic red-and-green bottle. Tabasco, the famous Louisiana pepper sauce, was founded in 1868 on nearby Avery Island. Bring binoculars for a closeup view of the "Tabasco" Last Supper. Blending Catholic and Cajun cultures (with a dash of humor), the medallion hangs high off the floor, near a stained glass window of the Eucharist.

Crown of Soot

On Ash Wednesday Eve 2016, a parishioner was passing by Our Lady of Guadalupe Church in tiny Conejos, Colorado, when he noticed smoke coming from inside. As providence (and perhaps Our Lady herself) had it, local firefighters were gathered for a meeting at the firehouse in Antonio, three miles down the road, when the 911 call came in. The first responders were on the scene within minutes, and the historic church was saved.

But the fire left behind smoke damage and a miraculous image. Before the fire, a large portrait of Our Lady of Guadalupe above the high altar wasn't wearing a crown. After the fire, a multi-pointed crown of soot appeared over her head, just like it belonged there. But then, Our Lady is Queen of Heaven and Earth and the very reason the church is even here.

According to parish lore, Hispano settlers from New Mexico were traveling through the area in 1854 when one of the burros in the pack train refused to take another step. Nothing, not bribes nor beatings, could make the stubborn beast go. When the men decided to lighten the burro's load, they discovered a small statue of Our Lady of Guadalupe in a pannier.

Taking this as a sign, the devout settlers promised to build a chapel to Our Lady on that very spot — and they did. Our Lady of Guadalupe Church is the oldest Catholic parish in Colorado. And the crown of soot? Our Lady is still wearing it today.

Wandering Minstrel

On September 5, 2008, a man who called himself the "Wandering Minstrel" appeared at St. Thomas the Apostle Catholic Church in Coeur d'Alene, Idaho. In exchange for a meal, he offered to patch and paint the stairwell in the parish center building, a former school. After he had finished his work and eaten a meal, the Minstrel gave a handcrafted cross to a parish employee and asked him to hang it in the freshly painted stairwell. The Minstrel also described his vision for a "Cove of Crosses."

Some days later, a beautiful crucifix arrived anonymously at the church. It was placed next to the Minstrel's cross. Then, dozens of crosses and crucifixes of every kind began arriving from around the globe, many with fascinating backstories. Who was this Wandering Minstrel? Nobody knows, but the stairwell he patched and painted was dedicated in 2017 as the Cove of Crosses Shrine.

Waiting with Mary

Mary waited … and waited … and waited to be born in artwork at Nativity of Blessed Virgin Mary Chapel in Flagstaff, Arizona. The Gothic stone chapel with pink concrete gargoyles was dedicated in 1930, but the wall behind the main altar stood blank for decades. One day in 1962, Mrs. Viola Babbitt, a Mormon-turned-Catholic, was lamenting to Stephen Juharos, a renowned artist living in nearby Sedona, how the blank wall needed art. The Hungarian native drew up a sketch of a proposed painting and gave it to the pastor.

For fifteen long years, Juharos (and Mary) waited for word about the painting. In 1978, Father Vincent Nevulis, the new pastor, found the sketch under the staircase in the rectory. He wanted the painting completed with haste! Juharos, now age sixty-five, rendered the floor-to-ceiling masterpiece in just six months. Titled *Presentation of the Newborn Baby Mary to the Rel-*

atives, the sixteen-by-thirty-five-foot work of art took five rolls of canvas and was installed in 1979. At long last, Mary was born — larger than life, even — at her namesake church.

Extreme Trivia QUESTION 8

I was born Thomas Merton in 1915. In 1941, I entered the Trappist Abbey of Gethsemani at Trappist, Kentucky, where I was ordained a priest and penned dozens of books, including the 1948 bestseller The Seven Storey Mountain. *I died in 1968 and was buried in the abbey cemetery. My grave marker gives my religious name. What was that name?*

Father's Day Church

When Edward B. Henslee's son was drafted into World War II, the Illinois lawyer made a pact with God. If Edward Jr. returned home alive, he vowed to personally finance and build a church in a town without a Catholic church — his small hometown of Dickson, Tennessee. The church would be dedicated to Saint Christopher, patron of travelers on perilous journeys. Henslee didn't wait for God's answer to his prayer; he began planning the church as an act of faith.

Saint Christopher brought Edward Jr. home safely, but building materials were scarce and sky-high in price after the war. Dickson was getting along well enough with Mass held in a local home, people told the lawyer. Wasn't that good enough? Not for Henslee. He stayed the course with the little redbrick church. Before long, others got caught up in his promise. Bishop William

L. Adrian of the Diocese of Nashville designed and carved the wooden altar. The bell came from a Lutheran church, the cherry paneling and fine woodwork from an old southern plantation home.

St. Christopher Catholic Church was dedicated on June 17, 1951 — Father's Day. There wasn't a dry eye in the church house.

Our Lord of the Rocket Ships

It's the Taj Mahal. It's a rocket silo. No, it's St. Joseph the Betrothed Ukrainian Catholic Church in Chicago, hailed as one of the world's most architecturally unique churches. The thirteen golden domes of the ultramodern Byzantine church, consecrated in 1977, represent Jesus and the Twelve Apostles. Rumor has it that international pilots use the domes to align their planes with the longest runway, number 10-28, at Chicago's O'Hare International Airport. When seen against a starry sky, the domes appear ready for liftoff. Maybe that's how the church got the sobriquet "Our Lord of the Rocket Ships."

A Palace Redeemed

In 1921, when the Ku Klux Klan bought the Greek Revival mansion with stately white columns in the Buckhead area of Atlanta, Georgia, people whispered about the secret goings-on inside the "Imperial Palace" — the Klan's national headquarters. Everyone knew that Hiram Wesley Evans, the Imperial Wizard, was out to destroy the American Catholic Church. But history winked, and by the mid-1920s, the Klan's power and wealth had collapsed. The palace was sold and resold a number of times. Nobody, it seems, could stay in the mansion for long.

In 1936, Bishop Gerald P. O'Hara of the Diocese of Savannah (the Diocese of Atlanta was created in 1956) bought the property for some $35,000 and erected the Cathedral of Christ the King in French Gothic style. It's said that O'Hara even invited the Imperial Wizard to the cathedral dedication in 1939. The Wizard was a no-show.

Stained Glass Miracle

The story of Immaculate Conception Catholic Church at Pawhuska, Oklahoma, reads like a fairytale. When oil was struck on Osage land around the turn of the twentieth century, the Osage tribe suddenly became the richest people per capita in the world. It's said that Osage men drove the finest cars (there was even a Rolls Royce dealership in town), and women strolled the streets in diamond-studded shoes. Osage oil money built the redbrick Gothic church, nicknamed the Cathedral of the Osage, and commissioned some of the country's finest stained glass windows. One window is a "double miracle," people say.

The Osage wanted to honor Father John Schoenmakers, the Jesuit priest who had brought Catholicism to the Osage in 1847, when the tribe was still living at Saint Paul, Kansas. But there was a problem: The proposed Osage Window depicted living tribal members, and the Vatican didn't allow living people to be portrayed in church windows. What's more, the Dutch-born priest hadn't achieved sainthood. The Osage appealed to the Vatican.

Miracle one: A special dispensation was granted for the window.

Working from photographs of the Osage, the Bavarian Art Glass Company in Munich, Germany, began crafting the now-famous window. Money was no object, and gold dust was added to achieve the most brilliant of reds. When World War I broke out, another story goes, the German artisans buried the masterpiece in the sandy bank of a river to protect it from shelling.

Miracle two: The window survived the war intact.

As soon as the Osage Window was installed at the Cathedral of the Osage, tourists from around the country began flocking to the small-town church. There's no window like it on earth.

Schoenmakers holds a cross as the Osage tribe, attired in native dress, listens to the Word of God. Tribal members depicted include Osage Chief Bacon Rind and his wife, Julia, Chief Saucy Calf, and Indian interpreter Arthur Bonnicastle and his wife. When parishioners gaze at the window, they're looking at their ancestors — ancestors who live on in stained glass.

Not Pig's Eye!

When Father Lucien Galtier arrived in 1840 at the river settlement of Pig's Eye, Minnesota, he surely grimaced. The name Pig's Eye was hardly filled with grace. Yet grace would flow. The priest erected a log chapel dedicated to St. Paul the Apostle, and Pig's Eye soon became known as Saint Paul. Good thing, too, or Pig's Eye — not Saint Paul — would be the state capital of Minnesota! In 1850, the Diocese of Saint Paul (now the Archdiocese of Saint Paul and Minneapolis) was formed, and the humble log church elevated to a frontier cathedral.

Opened in 1915, today's Cathedral of Saint Paul is literally a beacon on a hill. Designed by French architect Emmanuel Louis Masqueray, the magnificent stone church rises 306 feet to the heavens, a copper-clad lantern lit at night for all to see. Interestingly, Masqueray modeled the cathedral after St. Peter's Basilica in Rome — and not the Basilica of St. Paul Outside the Walls, also in Rome, where Saint Paul is buried.

Fishermen's Church

When Jesus called his apostles, they left their fishing nets and followed him. The apostles are back fishing again — this time with parishioners of St. Michael Catholic Church in Biloxi, Mississippi. The cylindrical church, with distinctive clam-shaped roof, features stories-tall stained glass windows of the apostles gathering in their catch. A scalloped clam roof also tops a tiny adjacent day chapel.

Come late spring, the apostles catch tourists by the boatloads during St. Michael's annual Blessing of the Fleet, a nearly century-old ritual held at the beginning of shrimping season. In earlier days, shrimping boats would line up in rows, and the priest would walk across the boats, bow to bow, blessing each and every one. One year, the priest lost his balance and fell into the drink, as they say. Now, the priest stands in an anchored "blessing boat," sprinkling the vessels with holy water as they parade by in colorful procession.

Smuggling Our Lady

Our Lady of Charity (*Nuestra Señora de la Caridad* in Spanish) at the National Shrine of Our Lady of Charity in Miami, Florida, was smuggled to freedom. During the summer of 1961, a Cuban priest in Miami asked his mother in Cuba to send him the statue of Our Lady of Charity — Cuba's patron saint — that he had commissioned for his parish church before being exiled. When communist dictator Fidel Castro rose to power in 1959, churches and statues were seized and desecrated. Some 1.4 million Cubans, including hundreds of priests, fled the island nation.

Smuggling plans were put in place. The sixteen-inch statue was secreted from the carver's workshop in Havana to a private Havana home to the Italian Embassy to the Panamanian embassy. The final handoff was to a Cuban political refugee seeking asylum in the United States. Toting the underground statue in a bag, the refugee boarded a flight for Miami. Cuba's "Statue of Liberty" arrived on American soil on September 8, the double feast of Our Lady of Charity and of the Nativity of Mary.

Preservation by Relocation

St. Gerard Church in Buffalo, New York, modeled after the Basilica of St. Paul Outside the Walls in Rome, was closed in 2008.

But St. Gerard's didn't give up the ghost. Many of its furnishings were moved 900 miles south to the newly built Mary Our Queen Catholic Church in Peachtree Corners, Georgia. If Mary Our Queen looks familiar, it is. As it so happened, Mary Our Queen has a blueprint similar to St. Gerard's.

Step inside Mary Our Queen, and you're also in St. Gerard's. St. Gerard's century-old stained glass windows, wooden pews, and high altar are all here. So are the baptismal font, the Pietà statue, confessional, and tabernacle. Mary Our Queen Church was dedicated in 2019, a new church with a historic past.

Extreme Trivia
QUESTION 9

Which American saint loved dancing so much that a church, designed in her honor, is reminiscent of a ballroom?

Church of the Frozen Chosen

Only the "frozen chosen" attend the Ice Masses at the Ice Chapel of Our Lady of the Snows in Houghton, Michigan. Every January since 2016, Catholic students at Michigan Technological University (MTU) and community members build a chapel of ice and packed snow at St. Albert the Great University Parish. The open-air chapel — bigger than many pioneer log churches — features an ice altar, "stained ice" windows (shards of colored ice), a snow pulpit, and a snow confessional.

The "coolest Mass" in America, the Ice Masses, especially the candlelit evening services, attract Catholic and non-Catholic students alike. Come spring, the chapel melts back into God's green earth. When winter rolls around again, a new Ice Chapel goes up in time for MTU's Winter Carnival in mid-February.

Ghost-Town Church

Set your clock back 125 years at Our Lady of Tears Catholic Church in Silver City, Idaho, an old gold and silver mining ghost town. Built in 1898, the hilltop frame structure started out as St. James Episcopal Church. When mining petered out in the 1920s and the town's population dwindled, speculators in nearby Nampa wanted to buy the building and turn it into a roadhouse. The Episcopal bishop wouldn't hear of it and sold the church for one dollar to the Catholic bishop. Periodic summer Masses are held in the picturesque white church, making Our Lady of Tears one of the few active ghost-town churches in the country.

Let There Be Light

In 1923, Thomas Edison lit up the Church of St. John the Evangelist in Orange, New Jersey. Legend holds that he personally supervised the installation of the church's first lights — twelve electric chandeliers. It's a wonder the church even lived to see the light of day. When Bishop Michael A. Corrigan became ordinary of the Diocese of Newark in 1873, the spectacular Victorian Gothic brownstone was a whopping $300,000 in debt ($8 million today). The indebtedness of this church alone threatened to bankrupt the diocese. The thirty-three-year-old Corrigan — the youngest bishop in US history — shot a prayer heavenward and then did the only thing he could: He ordered collections taken up in every Catholic church in New Jersey to save the church in Orange. St. John's lights are still on today.

Catechism on a Stick

When Indians of various tribes converged in 1839 near today's St. Francis Xavier Church at Toledo, Washington, to hear about the Great Spirit, Father (later Archbishop) François N. Blanchet found himself in a catechesis crisis. How to explain biblical history and the Catholic Faith to tribes who spoke different dialects? The French Canadian hit upon an ingenious idea: the Catholic Ladder.

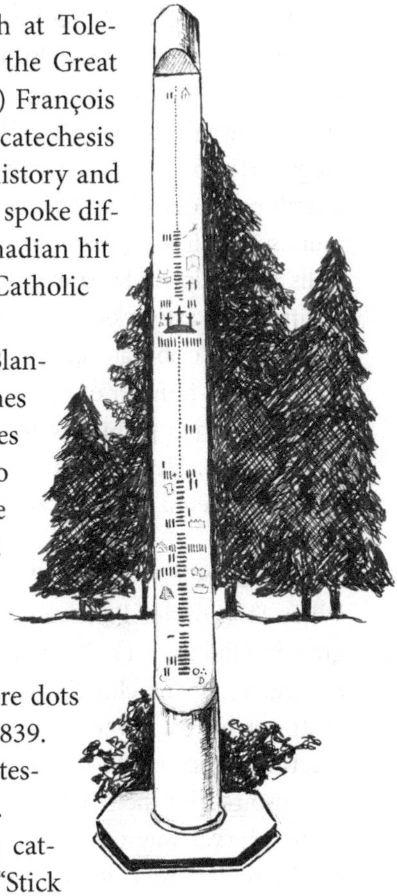

On a tall piece of wood, Blanchet notched forty horizontal lines to represent the forty centuries from the creation of the world to the birth of Christ. Thirty-three dots and three crosses signified Christ's thirty-three years on earth and his death and resurrection. Eighteen more horizontal lines and thirty-nine more dots brought the Ladder current, to 1839. A withered branch denoted Protestant defections from the Church.

Indians called the pictorial catechism the "Sahale Stick," or "Stick from Heaven." The Ladder proved so effective that Protestant missionaries adopted the evangelism tool but excised the withered branch. One Protestant Ladder even showed mitered heads falling into hellfire, but such were the times. A giant replica of the Catholic Ladder, resembling a totem pole of sorts, stands outside St. Francis Xavier Church. Another Catholic Ladder can be found inside St. Peter Catholic Mission at Suquamish, Washington. A Catholic convert, Chief Seattle, is buried in the adjacent cemetery.

Montana's "Sistine Chapels"

A handyman and a cook, Brother Joseph Carignano, SJ (1853–1919), one of America's most prolific artists, also "served up" church art. During a thirty-two-month period in the early 1900s, the self-taught artist from Turin, Italy, painted 124 murals — roughly four murals per month — in Montana's two "Sistine Chapels." Sixty-six murals, illuminating Bible stories and saintly characters, cover the walls and ceiling of St. Francis Xavier Church in Missoula. Another fifty-eight artworks adorn St. Ignatius Mission at St. Ignatius, including an elaborate apse triptych detailing the three visions of St. Ignatius, a founder of the Jesuit order.

Carignano's paintings are *egg-ceptionally* beautiful and for good reason: He made his own egg tempera paints. The artist-cook ordered (and cracked) eggs by the dozens.

Triple-Decker Church

When St. Aloysius Parish in downtown Detroit, Michigan, outgrew its church in 1930, it had a problem. How could the parish expand when the church, hemmed in by two buildings, had a footprint of just seventy-two feet by 100 feet? The answer: by erecting a "theater church" seating over 2,000.

Inspired by the Milan Cathedral in Italy, the neo-Romanesque marvel was designed with three tiers of seating and a semi-circular "well" in front of the high altar. Worshippers on the main tier view the Mass straight on; people seated in the three-quarters wraparound balcony look down; and churchgoers in the lower tier gaze up. Because everybody can see the priest no matter where they're seated, St. Al's got the moniker "Everybody's Church." There's not another triple-decker church like it in the world.

His and Her Churches

Richard C. Kerens (1842–1916) did something that no other

American can claim: He built "his and her" churches in honor of his parents. In 1904, Kerens erected St. Elizabeth of Hungary Catholic Church in Eureka Springs, Arkansas, in memory of his mother, Elizabeth. Famous for its walk-through bell tower, the charming stone church was featured three times in *Ripley's Believe It or Not* — in 1931, 1953, and 1961. Due to the steep terrain, visitors enter the church through the stand-alone bell tower.

In 1906, Kerens, a railroad developer and US ambassador to Austria-Hungary, built St. Thomas Catholic Church in Gassaway, West Virginia, to honor his father, Thomas. The rugged stone church with jaunty bell cot cost $30,000 ($1 million today) and is the oldest church in the small Blue Ridge Mountain town.

How Many Miles to Wall Drug (Chapel)?

You've seen the signs … "150 miles to Wall Drug" … "76 miles to Wall" … "Turn here!" What the signs don't say is that all roads lead to the Travelers Chapel at Wall Drug — the 76,000-square-foot tourist extravaganza at Wall, South Dakota. During the Great Depression, however, Wall Drug was another story: It had more flies than customers.

Ted and Dorothy Hustead bought the drugstore in 1931, attracted by Wall's small-town life and St. Patrick's Church that offered daily Mass. But Wall was in the middle of nowhere, and travelers saw little reason to pull into town. One sizzling hot day in July 1936, Dorothy was listening to the jalopies rumbling by Wall when inspiration hit. "Why not offer free ice water for travelers to stop?" And so, Ted erected the first signs advertising free ice water.

The rest, as they say, is history. Wall Drug expanded to become a major South Dakota attraction. In 1985, Ted and Dorothy's son, Bill, added the Travelers Chapel, a sanctuary for the road weary. Patterned after a Trappist chapel at New Melleray Abbey near Peosta, Iowa, the Travelers Chapel, with tall brick walls, is a mini oasis of rest. Best of all, the chapel's graces — like the ice water — are free.

Largest Stairway

For extra penance (and anointed exercise too), make the steep climb up the Mount of the Sacred Heart at the Mother Cabrini Shrine near Golden, Colorado. The sweeping view at the top is worth every step: all 373 of them! The Stairway of Prayer (the Stations of the Cross line the steps) is the largest Catholic stair-

way in the country. On the way down, stop at the spring for a refreshing cup of miracle water — a story with a Lourdes vibe to it.

When Mother Frances Cabrini, an Italian native and founder of the Missionary Sisters of the Sacred Heart of Jesus, bought the first parcel of land here in 1909, it was dirt cheap. It was said that no water was to be found on the land. Water for drinking and cooking had to be hauled up from a stream at the bottom of a canyon. In 1912, when several sisters complained of thirst, Mother walked the land and then tapped a large red rock with her cane. Turn it over and dig a hole, she told them. They did, and water began trickling forth. The spring is still running today.

Mother Cabrini became a naturalized US citizen in 1909. Just thirty-seven years later, on July 7, 1946, Mother became the first American citizen to be canonized a saint.

Come, Holy Ghost!

What has eight sides and is shaped like a queen's crown? The one and only Holy Ghost Mission at Kula, on the Hawaiian island of Maui. Built in 1894 by Portuguese immigrants from the Azores and Madeira Islands who had come to work the sugar plantations, the octagonal frame church is said to represent the eight-sided crown of St. Elizabeth of Portugal (1271–1336). The church is also noted for its annual Holy Ghost Feast, a tradition begun by Queen Elizabeth herself.

When a devastating drought hit the Azores in the 1300s, one legend goes, the starving Portuguese prayed to the Holy Ghost. On Pentecost Sunday, a ship carrying food arrived at a local port. When Queen Elizabeth heard of this great providence, she processed to the Lisbon cathedral and left her crown on the altar in thanksgiving. She also began the tradition of feeding the hungry on Pentecost. Seven centuries later, Holy Ghost Mission at Kula continues the queen's Holy Ghost Feast with a free laulau meal on Pentecost weekend.

Vermont's "Leper Church"

When Servant of God Joseph Dutton (1843–1931) landed in 1886 on the leper island of Molokai, Hawaii, the Civil War veteran told St. Damien de Veuster, "I have come to help." He stayed for the rest of his life. The story of Brother Joseph and Father Damien is told in twelve head-turning murals on the exterior of Blessed Sacrament Church half a world away in Stowe, Vermont. Dutton, a Catholic convert, was born on a farm where the church now stands.

Rendered by French artist André Girard, the wooden murals with black sticklike figures include Dutton's arrival at the leper colony, lepers with deformities receiving the sacraments, and Veuster's death from leprosy in 1889. Girard also decorated the interior of Blessed Sacrament Church, possibly the nation's only church painted inside and out by one artist.

Can't Find a Seat?

Can't find a seat at Sunday Mass? Build a bigger church! That's what Spanish immigrant Rafael Guastavino did in Asheville, North Carolina. In 1905, Guastavino — of New York City's Carnegie Hall and Grand Central Station architectural fame — began erecting the Basilica of Saint Lawrence, Deacon and Martyr, in Spanish Renaissance design. Guastavino's trademark building style is over your head, literally. Spanning fifty-eight by eighty-two feet, the dome — layers of terracotta tile embedded in layers of mortar — is considered the largest freestanding elliptical dome in America.

Guastavino, who died before the church was completed in 1909, rests in a church crypt. He now has his very own seat.

"Surround Sound"

Demons tremble when the Hazel Wright Organ at Christ Cathedral in Garden Grove, California, breaks into song. The fifth largest pipe organ in the world, "Hazel," as the glorious instrument is called, boasts more than 17,000 pipes, over 300 stops, and nearly 300 ranks. Hazel plays from all four corners of the church, giving Mass goers a surround-sound experience.

Christ Cathedral is a legend in itself. Built in 1977 by Protestant televangelist Robert H. Schuller, the glass structure was originally called Crystal Cathedral. The 78,397-square-foot megachurch (a football field is 57,600 square feet) is 120 feet tall, 141 feet long, and 207 feet wide, and was constructed entirely of glass — 10,660 panes of mirrored glass to be exact — and steel. The world-famous landmark seats 3,000, the population of a small California town.

The Diocese of Orange acquired the thirty-four-acre church campus for $57.5 million in 2012. Christ Cathedral may be the world's only Protestant megachurch-turned-Catholic cathedral.

Calling All Angels

Where do angels go sightseeing in Sin City — Las Vegas, Nevada? The Guardian Angel Cathedral, just off the Las Vegas Strip, of course. Everything about the cathedral, which opened in 1963, is dramatic and angelic — from a tall mosaic of a guardian angel over the front doors, to the A-shaped roof said to imitate angel wings folded in prayer, to the A-shaped stained glass windows. When the cathedral is filled to capacity with tourists at one of the weekend Masses, it's a sure bet 1,100 guardian angels are here too.

Brick Marvel

The town of Saint Paul, Oregon, shook and rattled on March 25, 1993, but the Scott Mills earthquake (also dubbed the Mount Angel earthquake) couldn't take down St. Paul Church — Oregon's oldest Catholic church. That the 1846 structure even survived the 5.6 magnitude quake is no small marvel: The five-brick-thick walls had no mortar or cement holding the 60,000 bricks together!

To preserve the historic church — believed the oldest brick building in the Pacific Northwest — the redbrick walls were taken down in sections, replaced with concrete blocks reinforced with steel, and then faced with the original bricks. St. Paul Church now stands tall and ready to take on the world, even another "Angel" earthquake.

Extreme Trivia QUESTION 10

Visit the Four Corners Monument near Teec Nos Pos, Arizona, and you're not only standing in four states at once, but visiting three dioceses as well. Name the three dioceses.

Seating a Whole Town

Where can a whole town fit inside the local Catholic church? At the Basilica of St. Fidelis in Victoria, Kansas. When German émigrés from Russia erected the Romanesque stone church in 1908–11, they built it big enough for everyone. Seating 1,100, the "Cathedral of the Plains," as it's called, can accommodate the town's entire population of 1,149 residents — if mothers hold their babies in their laps. The basilica is so grand and so beautiful that it was named one of the 8 Wonders of Kansas. No small wonder, indeed.

"I Have a Dream" Church

Decades before the Reverend Martin Luther King Jr. gave his famous "I Have a Dream" speech in 1963, Father Harold Purcell also had a dream: to ease the wretched poverty and downtrodden lives of blacks in the segregated South. In 1934, he began the City of St. Jude at Montgomery, Alabama, a thirty-six-acre complex that included St. Jude's Catholic Church, a medical clinic, and a school. Two of King's children were born at St. Jude's Catholic Hospital, the region's first racially integrated hospital.

On March 24, 1965, the City of St. Jude hosted the "Stars for Freedom Rally" on the eve of the historic fifty-four-mile march from Selma to Montgomery, which paved the way for the Voting Rights Act of 1965. Some 25,000 activists — bolstered in spirit by entertainers such as Sammy Davis Jr., Joan Baez, and Lena Horne — camped overnight on the grounds. Part of the Selma to Montgomery National Historic Trail, the City of St. Jude Interpretive Center tells the story of St. Jude's role in securing voting rights for all Americans, regardless of race.

Nerves of Steel

The Cathedral of the Holy Spirit in Bismarck, North Dakota, is a rare bird: The art deco structure is the only American cathedral dedicated to the Paraclete. In the early 1940s, Bishop Vincent J. Ryan asked farmers to donate the profit from one acre of land — "God's Acre" it was called — or a proportionate amount for workers in other occupations to fund the monolithic concrete church. The 163-foot tower was as tall as God's Acre allowed.

Some say it was the bishop's nerves of steel that built the cathedral. Ground was broken in September 1941, three months before America entered World War II. Concrete was not considered part of the war effort, but steel was. Yet the steel roof beams — shipped to Bismarck before the war — were never commandeered. How's that? The beams were hidden in the tall grasses of a slough! One day, when the cathedral walls had reached their full height, the steel roof beams appeared seemingly out of nowhere, and the building was enclosed.

In another interesting note, the cathedral opened on August 30, 1945, three days before V-J Day on September 2, which officially marked the end of World War II.

Grotto Recipe

You won't find this recipe in any church cookbook. Mix 125 sacks of cement, twenty tons of sand, sixty-four tons of local rock, three tons of decorative rock, four and one-half tons of brick, and one rock from the Calista Catacombs at Rome, and what do you get? A Byzantine grotto. At least that's what Father Peter N. Scheier got when he erected St. Peter's Grotto on the grounds of St. Peter's School in tiny Farmer, South Dakota.

Dedicated to the Virgin Mary, St. Peter's Grotto measures thirteen and one-half feet square. Turrets decorate the four corners, and an open-air cupola lights up Mary's three altars inside. Why was the grotto designed in a Byzantine style — a unique architectural form for a man-made cave? Only the folk artist knows for sure, and he's long gone to his heavenly reward.

There's one ingredient that Scheier didn't include in his grotto recipe: loads and loads of sweat. It took the artist seven years, begining in 1927, to build the quaint stone marvel on the prairie. St. Peter's School is no more, but St. Peter's Grotto stands as solid as the rock of Saint Peter.

Welcome Lady

Our Lady welcomes you to the State of Delaware in the tallest "welcome sign" in the land. Standing thirty-three-feet high, Our Lady Queen of Peace at Holy Spirit Church in New Castle greets motorists crossing the Delaware Memorial Bridge from New Jersey into northeast Delaware. And what a welcome sight she is. Her mantle and gown of welded strips of stainless steel reflect a silvery aura during the day, at dawn and dusk a celestial gold. When there's a full moon, she appears out of this world.

The work of renowned sculptor Charles C. Parks, Our Lady Queen of Peace Shrine was dedicated in 2007. The shrine exudes a heavenly calm — and no wonder. The faithful prayed more than 500,000 Rosaries for the money to fund the statue. That's 26.5 million Hail Marys!

Ugliest Saint Statue

The Father Damien Statue, greeting visitors to Hawaii's State Capitol in Honolulu, is the ugliest saint statue in America. Even Marisol Escobar, its artist, said the seven-foot bronze sculpture was ugly. But leprosy wasn't pretty, and neither was St. Damien de Veuster when he died of the disease in 1889, at age forty-nine. The Belgium native spent sixteen years caring for exiled lepers on the Hawaiian island of Molokai before succumbing to the disease himself.

Based on photos near his life's end, the boxy, modernist statue shows the disfigured holy man with leprosy scars on his face, his right hand in a sling, and stout shoes on his diseased feet. The ugly statue is beautiful in spirit, however, capturing the way in which the saint loved his fellow lepers to the very end.

A bronze copy of Father Damien's statue also graces National Statuary Hall at the US Capitol in Washington, DC, only one of two canonized American saints so honored. The other saint statue, executed by Ettore Cadorin, portrays Spanish Franciscan missionary Junípero Serra, who founded nine of California's twenty-one missions.

A Great Work

In 1892, little Peter Mayer's mother lay dying after giving birth to a baby girl. Terrified at the thought of losing his mother, the nine-year-old lad ran to his parish church in Kitchener, Ontario,

Canada, and cried his eyes out before a statue of Mother Mary. "Save my mother," he begged, "and I promise to do a great work for the Church." Both mother and baby lived. Peter later became a Servite priest and took the name Ambrose.

In 1923, Father Ambrose was serving in Portland, Oregon. His promise to Mary ever on his mind, he bought a tract of land: sixty-two acres of pristine wilderness. He then began carving out a massive cave-grotto at the base of a 110-foot-tall basalt cliff. Dedicated in 1924, the Sanctuary of Our Sorrowful Mother — measuring about thirty feet wide, thirty feet deep, and fifty feet high — is one of the biggest man-made caves ever. It is indeed a "great work."

The Grotto, as it's commonly called, ranks among the most popular attractions in the Pacific Northwest. All because a little boy cried out to his Mother Mary in heaven.

Dragon Doors

The most dramatic doors in America just might be the wood-carved "dragon doors" at St. Mary's Church in Boise, Idaho. The jaw-dropping artistry of J. Chester Armstrong, the nine-foot-by-sixteen-foot doors of Honduran mahogany are based on the Book of Revelation and depict St. Michael the Archangel slaying a seven-headed dragon. The dragon is no lightweight, either; the double doors weigh approximately 2,000 pounds each.

Carved in relief twelve to eighteen inches deep, the toothy dragon heads appear to lurch at parishioners entering the church. Fear not, Saint Michael to the rescue: One dragon head, which straddles the two doors, is lopped off every time the door is opened.

"Shoe Shrines"

In the American Southwest, it's believed the *Santo Niño* (Holy Child) walks the countryside at night, healing sick children and

wearing out his shoes on his peregrinations. Offerings of shoes, both in petition and in thanksgiving, are made at "shoe shrines" around the region, including the historic Santo Niño de Atocha Chapel at Chimayó, New Mexico. Handknit baby booties, wee tennis shoes, ballerina slippers, and tiny cowboy boots adorn the Santo Niño statue. Little shoes even line the adobe walls and ceiling.

Seated in a chair, the Santo Niño statue evokes wonder. Pilgrims often report finding the Child's sandal-shod feet dusty, as though he had just returned from a long trip.

Miracle Jesus

When a wicked fire in 1895 devoured Saint Anthony of Padua Catholic Church in Jersey City, New Jersey, people wept — until they saw the miracle. The only object not touched by fire was a larger-than-life wooden crucifix over the main altar. The parish rebuilt the magnificent Victorian Gothic brownstone church, the Mother Church of Polonia in New Jersey, and enshrined the Miraculous Crucifix in a side chapel. No fire could take out their Lord.

\+ + + + +

On October 8, 1871, the Great Peshtigo Fire — the deadliest fire in American history — barreled across northeast Wisconsin. Some 1,500 to 2,000 souls perished in the great fireball. Father Peter Pernin, pastor of St. Mary's Church in Peshtigo, ran to the church and rescued the wooden tabernacle with the Blessed Sacrament. Pernin loaded the tabernacle into a wagon and then pushed the wagon into the Peshtigo River. He then jumped into the river to save himself.

The entire town burned to the ground.

Three days later, wrote Pernin in *The Finger of God Is There!*, the tabernacle, painted a snowy white, was found floating on a log. The tabernacle showed no signs of damage, not even charring. When Pernin opened the tabernacle door, he gasped. The monstrance with Host was perfectly intact! The ciborium hadn't been disturbed either.

The Miracle Tabernacle can still be seen in Peshtigo today.

Born-Again Stone

From slave stone to font of eternal life — that's the legacy of the baptismal font at the Abbey Basilica of Mary Help of Christians at Belmont, North Carolina. When Benedictine monks settled here in 1876, they named the site Mariastein (Mary's Stone) in honor of the Blessed Virgin Mary and for a large granite boulder on the property. Tradition holds the stone was once used as a slave auction block.

In the 1960s, the old slave stone was made into a baptismal font and placed inside the basilica. A brass legend reads, "Upon this rock, men once were sold into slavery. Now upon this rock, through the waters of Baptism, men become free children of God."

Disappearing Cross

Want to see Jesus? He appears nightly at St. Francis de Sales Church in Purcellville, Virginia. Every night, from dusk to dawn, the *Crux Gloria* (Glorious Cross) — a thirty-three-foot-tall steel cross with a cutout figure of Jesus — turns into an apparition. When the cutout is illuminated from within, the 17,000-pound cross fades away and Jesus' body appears suspended in air, often bringing motorists to a screeching halt.

"Good Lord!" they exclaim. "Is that Jesus?"

Metal sculptor Tomás José Fernández got the idea for the cross in 1988 when, he claims, Jesus appeared to him in a vision and said, "My Cross is a Cross of Light."

Extreme Trivia QUESTION 11

I won an Emmy Award for my television show Life is Worth Living *and was bi-ritual, that is, I could offer Mass in both the Roman Catholic and Byzantine traditions. Who am I? (Hint: A famous actor adopted my surname.)*

Requiem for a President

The Cathedral of St. Matthew the Apostle in Washington, DC, will be forever remembered in American history: The Requiem Mass for slain President John F. Kennedy, the country's first Catholic president, was held here on November 25, 1963. A marble floor plaque, in front of the sanctuary gates, marks the spot where his remains rested. Outside, in front of the stately redbrick church, three-year-old John F. Kennedy Jr. saluted his father's flag-draped casket, a farewell gesture that captivated a mourning nation.

Cathedral by the (Big) Numbers

Numbers don't lie: The Cathedral Basilica of the Sacred Heart of Jesus in Newark, New Jersey, ranks among America's greatest churches. Fifty-five years passed from the laying of the cornerstone (1899) to the dedication (1954), and the French Gothic stone beauty is 365 feet long (one foot for every day of the year), comparable in size to London's Westminster Abbey. Some 200 stained glass windows, crafted of pot glass in medieval style, decorate the interior. The Great Rose Window, thirty-six feet in diameter, is the largest rose window of any Catholic church in the Western Hemisphere.

What makes the mother church of New Jersey so fabulous is that everyone — believer or not — who passes through the massive front doors gets a free spiritual trip. Because the cathedral is designed on the vertical (no horizontal lines), people's eyes and hearts are whisked to the heavens. Still not wowed? In another bragging right, the 232-foot twin towers are taller than those of the famed Notre-Dame Cathedral in Paris, France.

Statuesque Rebuttal

During the 1870s, a newspaper in Honolulu, Hawaii, accused Catholics of worshiping statues as idols. Bishop Louis-Désiré

Maigret, SS.CC, responded in kind: He ordered thirty-six French statuettes and placed them on Gothic arches overlooking the nave of the Cathedral Basilica of Our Lady of Peace. A holy roundup of patriarchs, prophets, and saints — from Abraham to Jeremiah to the Twelve Apostles to Saints Jerome and Teresa of Ávila — the statuettes provided a short course of important figures in biblical and Church history. They were also used to instruct the faithful on the proper veneration of statues and relics. The 150-year-old polychrome figures still inhabit the cathedral today.

Dime-a-Week Cathedral

In the 1870s, Father Daniel Mullen, a Civil War chaplain, found a way for his flock of poor Irish immigrants to build St. Patrick's Church in Norwich, Connecticut — in the town's Millionaires' District of all places. His plan: a dime a week. Even that was a sacrifice. An unskilled worker or domestic servant might earn $1.33 per day. Coffee costs twelve cents per pound, a bushel of wheat, $1.02, not to mention rent or clothing. It's said the hard-working Irish pinched their pennies so hard they turned into dimes. The Gothic Revival church was dedicated in 1879.

Irish eyes were smiling in heaven and on earth when the Diocese of Norwich was formed in 1953 and the dime-a-week church was elevated to the Cathedral of St. Patrick. Never were dimes better spent.

Angel Doors

Before Mass goers even set foot inside Saint Thomas Aquinas Cathedral in Reno, Nevada, they're blessed. Covered with Nevada copper, the main doors depict two embossed angels incensing the faithful as they enter the 1906 neoclassical church. At night, it's said the one of a kind copper angels turn forward and heap incense upon the city and the Diocese of Reno.

Section Three

INCREDIBLE PEOPLE OF FAITH

Stories of incredible Catholics in America are legion. There's simply not enough room to begin to tell the stories of all the great men, women, and children. The standout personalities in this section all have one thing in common: They are the first in some way, among the sainted elite in another, or extraordinary in yet another way.

Did you know that the first woman in America to become a nun was born a Puritan? Or that the Good Thief has his own post office? Hailed as America's protomartyr, Padre Juan de Padilla died in 1542, a century before the three North American Martyrs were slain in New York. Other larger-than-life personalities in this section include an actor who was crucified over 9,000 times and a nun who had a "hell of a will" and meant it.

A Maine Hero

St. John's Church in Bangor, Maine, preserves a horrific episode of American Catholic persecution: The tarring and feathering of Father Johannes Bapst (1815–1887), a Swiss Jesuit.

In January 1853, the thirty-seven-year-old priest took up residence in Ellsworth, Maine, where his Sunday afternoon lectures on the Catholic Faith won many converts and incited the wrath of the town's Know-Nothings — a nativist party that claimed to "know nothing" of attacks on Catholic immigrants and churches. According to Jesuit annals, the Know-Nothings denounced Bapst "from the pulpit and in the press, as a perverter of the young" and warned that he would suffer injury if he continued proselytizing.

Bapst stayed put.

That fall, when Catholic students were expelled from an Ellsworth public school for refusing to read the Protestant Bible in class or join in Protestant prayers, Bapst decided to open a parochial school in an old chapel. The Know-Nothings bombed the schoolhouse.

On the evening of June 3, 1854, a horde of Know-Nothings — dressed in white robes and wearing masks — descended on Bapst's home to wreak vengeance upon him. When they discovered the priest was out on a sick call, they smashed the windows instead. Several days later, the bigots attacked Ellsworth's St. Joseph Church. For his protection, Bapst was reassigned to Bangor.

Four months later, on Saturday, October 14, 1854, Bapst was traveling to a sick call in another town when he stopped in Ellsworth to hear confessions and offer Sunday Mass. Someone tipped off the Know-Nothings, and that night a mob — reportedly 500 strong — surrounded the home where he was staying. Afraid for the family's safety, Bapst climbed out of his cellar hiding spot and gave himself up to the crowd. The bigots stripped, tarred, and feathered the priest. He was then ridden on a rail through Ellsworth and left for dead at the town wharf. When he came to, Bapst wandered in a stupor back into town, where parish men picked the tar and feathers off his body.

After offering Mass on Sunday and Monday — guarded by men with pitchforks, it's said — Bapst left Ellsworth and never returned. Back in Bangor, he began erecting St. John's Church in late 1854. Placed under the cornerstone was a small bottle containing a piece of the priest's tarred, feathered, and bloodied cassock. It is believed that Bapst was the only priest in American history to be assaulted in such a heinous way.

Despite nativist threats to burn down the Bangor church, it stands today in all its neo-Gothic splendor and glory. John Bapst Memorial High School in Bangor is named in Bapst's honor, as is Bapst Library at Boston College in Boston, Massachusetts, where he served as its first president.

Extreme Trivia
QUESTION 12

In 1968, a bishop composed a witty prayer for a new National Football League team in his diocese. An excerpt of the prayer reads, "Our Heavenly Father ... grant our [name of team] an increase in faith and strength so that they will not only overcome the Lions, but also the Bears, the Rams, the Giants, and even those awesome people in Green Bay." Name the football team.

Mother Joseph the Carpenter

She wore a hammer tucked into her black belt along with a black rosary. She was fundraiser, architect, construction supervisor,

carpenter, woodcarver, and bricklayer. Who was this tall, angular woman who pinned up her long black dress and bounced on rafters to test their structural integrity? Mother Joseph of the Sacred Heart, SP (1823–1902).

Born Esther Pariseau near Montreal, Canada, the builder-whiz entered the Sisters of Providence in Montreal in 1843. Her father, a carriage-maker, accompanied the twenty-year-old to the convent doors and told the mother superior, "She can read, write, figure accurately, sew, cook, spin, and do all manner of housework. She can even do carpentering, handling a hammer and saw as well as her father."

And then some.

In 1856, Mother Joseph led a band of five Sisters of Providence from Montreal to Vancouver in Washington Territory. Then, the building spree began. Over the next four decades, Mother Joseph the Carpenter designed, built, or helped found at least ten hospitals, including the first hospital in the Pacific Northwest, as well as a number of schools and orphanages across a vast region that today encompasses Washington, northern Oregon, Idaho, and western Montana.

Her begging tours to raise money are the stuff of legends. Riding horseback from mining camp to mining camp, the intrepid nun appealed to lucky prospectors, often raising between $2,000 and $5,000 on a single tour. Once, highwaymen tried to steal Mother's black bag, plump with donations. She fended them off with a ruse: "There is nothing in there that you would want." They believed her! Indians called Mother the "Chief of the Lady Black Robes" (the Sisters of Providence).

Because funds were always tight, Mother's architectural designs were practical, the only frill her trademark belfry. Her finest building, still standing, is Providence Academy in Vancouver, Washington, a three-story brick affair erected in 1873. It's said that Mother personally inspected every brick used in its construction.

Mother's spirit lives today. A bronze statue of God's architect (praying, not hammering) graces National Statuary Hall in Washington, DC. The State of Washington celebrates April 16, her birthday, as Mother Joseph Day. Even the National Cowgirl Museum and Hall of Fame honors the plucky nun. The pioneer builder rests in Mother Joseph Catholic Cemetery of Vancouver, the country's only cemetery named for a carpenter-nun.

Protomartyr

Padre Juan de Padilla (1500–1542) was an extraordinary man. In 1541, the Spanish Franciscan missionary accompanied Francisco Vázquez de Coronado on his search for the fabled Seven Cities of Gold and wound up in Kansas. No gold was to be found on the tall-grass prairie, and the expedition spent twenty-five days among the Quivira Indians before returning to New Mexico.

The following year, Padilla went back to Kansas, a circuitous journey by foot of 1,000 miles, to evangelize the natives. He settled among the Quivira, who lived in villages of grass lodges, and taught them the Gospel. At some point, Padilla decided to leave the Quivira to evangelize other tribes and enlarge his tent of souls for the Lord. It's said the Quivira were outraged at Padilla's leave-taking; they had grown to love the "white chief." A day or so later, the Quivira (some sources claim it was another tribe) caught up with Padilla on the trail.

The padre, aware of what was to come, ordered his party to flee. As Padilla knelt down and offered up his life as a sacrifice for the salvation of the natives, a hail of arrows struck and killed him — a century before the martyrdoms of St. Isaac Jogues and companions in New York. Legend holds America's protomartyr was buried under a mountain of stones, but nobody knows for sure where. The Coronado Quivira Museum in Lyons, Kansas, captures the fascinating story.

"Michelangelo of the Capitol"

How does one go from Vatican artist to muralist at the US Capitol? Get exiled by a pope! Constantino Brumidi (1805–1880) was restoring frescoes at the Vatican in late 1848 when a revolution broke out in Rome, and Pope Pius IX had to flee the Eternal City. The artist was also a captain in the papal civil guard. But Brumidi, the story goes, couldn't bring himself to order guns turned on the rebels. Instead, he rescued priceless works of art from convents and monasteries and had them stored at the Lateran Palace for safekeeping.

Pope Pius IX returned to Rome in 1850. A year later, Brumidi, who had painted the pontiff's official portrait, was arrested for allegedly stealing artworks and other convoluted charges. Despite many affidavits proving his innocence, Brumidi was sentenced to eighteen years in prison. In 1852, the pope pardoned Brumidi and reportedly ordered him to leave Italy, never to return.

Upon arriving in America, Brumidi painted private portraits and decorated houses before landing the muralist job at the US Capitol in 1855. (He also rendered altarpieces and paintings for Catholic churches. The enormous Crucifixion at the Shrine of The Holy Innocents in New York City is hailed a masterpiece.) His capitol works include the *Apotheosis of Washington* and the *Frieze of American History*.

In 2012, the "Michelangelo of the Capitol" was posthumously awarded the Congressional Gold Medal.

First Black Bishop

As the Great Boston Fire of 1872 roared toward St. James Church in Boston, Massachusetts, legend holds a priest walked toward the inferno with a prayer book and prayed. Suddenly, the winds reversed, and the church was spared. Who was this man of great faith? Father James A. Healy, who would become the nation's first bishop of African descent. (Venerable Augustus Tolton, a former slave, is hailed as America's first black priest.)

The eldest of ten children, James Augustine Healy was born in 1830 near Macon, Georgia, to Michael Healy, an Irish immigrant cotton planter, and Eliza Clark, a mixed-race slave. Under Georgia antebellum law, children born of a slave mother were also slaves. Because slaves — lighter skinned, like James was, or not — were banned from attending school, Michael Healy sent his brood to the free North to be educated.

James attended Quaker schools and then the Jesuit College of the Holy Cross in Worcester, Massachusetts. Newly opened, the college was not strictly a postsecondary school and enrolled students at various grade levels. Soon after arriving in 1844, fourteen-year-old James and his three younger brothers were baptized. James later wrote, "Then, I was nothing; now I am Catholic."

James graduated valedictorian of his class in 1849. He then attended Sulpician seminaries in Montreal, Canada, and Paris, France, where he was ordained in 1854. Father Healy served the Church in Boston until 1875, when he was consecrated the second bishop of the Diocese of Portland, which then encompassed all of Maine and New Hampshire. Healy helped found the Diocese of Manchester, New Hampshire, in 1884.

When racism surfaced, Healy was known to engage with both tact and wit. A woman told how, as a young girl, the bishop was hearing her confession when she stopped mid-sentence. "I can't tell you the rest of my sins," the girl quavered, "I said something against you, Bishop."

"What did you say?" he asked.

"I said the bishop's as black as the devil!"

Stifling a chuckle, the prelate (who was so light-skinned he could pass for a white man) replied, "You can say he's as black as coal, or as black as the ace of spades, but don't say he's as black as the devil!"

Healy died in 1900, at age seventy. As he requested, he was interred in Calvary Cemetery in South Portland and not in a stately cathedral crypt. A tall Celtic cross honoring his Irish heritage marks the grave.

For God and Country

When Japan attacked Pearl Harbor, Hawaii, at 7:48 a.m. on December 7, 1941, the "day of infamy" also became a day of heroic grace. US Navy Chaplain Father Aloysius H. Schmitt had just finished saying Sunday Mass aboard the USS *Oklahoma* when torpedoes capsized the battleship. Instead of saving himself, the thirty-two-year-old Iowa native began pushing trapped men through a small porthole to safety. The chaplain and 428 shipmates perished that day. Schmitt became the first American chaplain of any faith to die in World War II.

In 2016 — seventy-five years after Pearl Harbor — Schmitt's remains were identified with DNA technology and reinterred at Christ the King Chapel at Loras College in Dubuque, Iowa, his alma mater. It was a fitting tribute; the school's motto is *Pro Deo et Patria* (For God and Country). Dedicated in Schmitt's honor in 1947, the chapel holds his chalice and prayerbook rescued from the *Oklahoma* wreckage. When found, the prayerbook was marked with a ribbon for the following day, December 8 — the sixth anniversary of his ordination as a priest.

Font of Courage

Father Aloysius H. Schmitt was the first chaplain of any denomination to die in World War II, and Father Thomas M. Conway (1908–1945) was the last. On July 30, 1945, the USS *Indianapolis* was crossing the Philippine Sea when a Japanese submarine fired two torpedoes. In less than twelve minutes, the heavy cruiser sank. More than 300 of the 1,195 men on board went down with the ship. For three days in shark-infested waters, Chaplain Lieutenant Conway swam from one group of surviving shipmates to another, offering absolution, baptism, and hope they would be rescued. He held dying sailors in his arms until they breathed their last.

Exhausted from no food or water, Conway succumbed on August 2. He was thirty-seven years old. About an hour after Conway's death, a Navy plane spotted the men at sea. Some believe it was the chaplain's spirit who guided the pilot to the scene. Of the 880 men who survived the torpedo attack, only 316 lived to be rescued. Conway was credited with saving the lives of at least sixty-seven men. Only God knows how many souls he ushered into heaven.

In 2015, a stunning memorial honoring Conway's heroism was installed on grounds of the Basilica of the Immaculate Conception in Waterbury, Connecticut. Sculpted by decorated Vietnam War veteran Andrew Chernak, the "font of courage" depicts Conway, a Waterbury native, in a circle of blue water holding a dying sailor aloft with his left hand, dog tags and a rosary in the other. In 2021, Conway was posthumously awarded the Navy Cross, the Navy's second highest award.

Gold Rush Priest

If Patrick Manogue (1831–1895) wasn't the first gold rush prospector to become a priest, the six-foot, four-inch, 250-pound Irishman arbitrated arguments like no other — sometimes with a pious punch! After prospecting enough gold to pay for his tuition, Manogue sailed to France and enrolled at Saint-Sulpice

Seminary in Paris. Ordained in 1861 at age thirty, the priest's first assignment was St. Mary in the Mountains in the silver and gold mining boomtown of Virginia City, Nevada.

And then the tall stories began.

When a dying Irish woman wanted the last rites, Manogue rode horseback twenty miles at night to her outback cabin. The woman's husband met Manogue at the front door, stuck a pistol in his face, and snarled, "No 'catlicker' priest is going near my wife." The bear-of-a-priest grabbed the man's pistol with one hand, knocked him down like a feather with the other, and walked on in. When wives said their husbands were frittering wages on drink or games of chance, "Father Hulk" just happened to appear at the payment office on payday to walk the errant husband home. He christened his first two Indian converts Adam and Eve.

Consecrated bishop in 1881, Manogue founded the Diocese of Sacramento, California, in 1886. Then, the "rush" was on to build Sacramento's Cathedral of the Blessed Sacrament. But the bishop didn't rush fast enough. When the Italian Renaissance structure was dedicated on June 30, 1889, artists were still painting the frescoes as people were arriving for the opening Mass.

Manogue died on Ash Wednesday, February 27, 1895, at age sixty-three. Tales of the Gold Rush priest — tales as tall as the cathedral steeple itself — filled the local papers for days.

Remembering Catholic Abe

Abraham Lincoln was Catholic. No, not President Abraham Lincoln, but his first cousin Abraham. There was a third Abraham Lincoln — their grandfather. Around 1780, Grandfather Abe moved his family from Virginia to Kentucky. His oldest son, Mordecai, won the hand of Mary Mudd, a Catholic, who gave birth to Abraham in 1797. Another son, Thomas, married Nancy Hanks and also had a son named Abraham, in 1809. This Abraham Lincoln would become the sixteenth president of the United States.

In 1830, both Mordecai and Thomas and their families were living in Illinois — now known as the Land of Lincoln. Mordecai settled near Fountain Green in Hancock County, where son Catholic Abe served as a township justice of the peace. Like his cousin Honest Abe, he was known as upright and just. Catholic Abe, his wife, and other relatives who make up the lost Catholic branch of the Lincoln family rest in St. Simon Cemetery, a secluded burial plot surrounded by private land near Fountain Green. A marker giving the cemetery's history can be seen from the road.

The Incorruptibles

Sister Wilhemina Lancaster, OSB (1924–2019), caused quite a national stir when her body was exhumed on April 28, 2023, at Abbey of Our Lady of Ephesus in rural Gower, Missouri. Her body appeared incorrupt. Then again, the African American nun didn't necessarily conform to conventional ways and was known to quip, "I am Sister Wil-hel-mina — I've a HELL of a WILL and I MEAN IT!"

The indomitable Wilhemina was born Mary Elizabeth Lancaster on Palm Sunday, 1924, in St. Louis, Missouri. After graduating from high school, she entered the Oblate Sisters of Providence — the world's first black order of nuns — in Baltimore, Maryland. When the order forsook the traditional religious habit after Vatican II, Wilhemina made her own habit and headdress, turning a plastic bleach bottle into a "starched guimpe." She also regretted the loss of the Latin Mass. When she couldn't convince the Oblates to resume their traditional ways, the seventy-year-old nun packed her bags and founded, in 1995, the Benedictines of Mary, Queen of Apostles.

Wilhemina died in 2019, at age ninety-five, and was buried in a simple wooden coffin. She was not embalmed. Four years later, her Benedictine daughters decided to exhume her remains for transfer to the abbey church. Her coffin was falling apart, but not Wilhemina or her black Benedictine habit; she looked as though she was simply taking a long nap. Her mortal remains were placed in a special glass case inside the abbey church in a shrine to Saint Joseph.

But Wilhemina can't necessarily claim the title of America's first incorruptible. That honor may belong to Bishop Richard Pius Miles (1791–1860), a Dominican and the first bishop of Tennessee. Could his incorrupt status be a serendipitous play on names? When Miles took the Dominican habit around 1809, he also took the name Pius, for Pope St. Pius V, who is incorrupt.

When Miles arrived on the Tennessee frontier in 1838, he was not only bishop but the only priest in the whole state! Setting out to meet his flock, the shepherd discovered some 300 Catholics scattered across Tennessee, most of whom hadn't seen a priest in decades, if ever. One eighty-year-old man waited thirty years to receive the Eucharist.

When Miles died in 1860, Tennessee counted thirteen priests, fourteen churches, six chapels, a seminary, three communities of religious sisters, nine parochial schools, and 12,000 Catholics. God's servant was buried in a cast iron casket beneath the altar of Nashville's St. Mary of the Seven Sorrows Church. During a church renovation in 1972, the bishop's body was exhumed — 112 years after his death — and found to be incorrupt. He was reinterred in a tomb in a rear chapel of the church.

According to urban legend, the good bishop isn't resting at all. Some workers in downtown Nashville claim there are times when St. Mary's bells fail to ring as scheduled. The spirit of Bishop Miles, they say, is letting them know that a life without God isn't a life at all.

Lost (and Found) Sheep of Catholic Hill

If the walls of St. James the Greater Mission near Walterboro,

South Carolina, could talk, you'd hear one of the greatest faith stories in America. Irish planters built the first church in 1833, at what locals called "Catholic Hill." As was the custom, plantation slaves adopted the religion of their masters. The Lowcountry church burned in 1856, but for whatever reason (perhaps the impending Civil War) it was not rebuilt. When slavery was abolished in 1865, the Irish abandoned the land, leaving the freed slaves without priest or church.

If the Church forgot the blacks at Catholic Hill, the blacks didn't forget the Church. The rural enclave kept holy the Lord's Day, meeting and praying in common. Babies were baptized into the kingdom of God. Couples jumped the broomstick to get married. For thirty long years, the band clung to their Catholic Faith and to an African proverb: "However long the night may last, there will be morning."

Morning came in 1892, when Father Daniel Berberich was traveling through the area and happened upon the lost colony. A church went up and then a two-story school for black children. The current church, faced with wooden shingles painted red, was erected in the mid-1930s with a "priest's room," where itinerant priests bedded overnight when they came to offer Mass.

If a black Catholic parish was a rarity in the rural Deep South, even rarer still was the graveyard at St. James the Greater Mission. It's biracial. The oldest grave belongs to a white man, Irish-born James McKain, who died in 1835. Other graves hold the remains of slaves and freed slaves. Born a slave in 1806, Diana Bolen died a free woman in 1899.

"Good Thief Post Office"

May 30, 2023, was a red-letter day in Herington, Kansas. By an act of the US Congress, the small-town post office, noted for its 1937 New Deal mural, was officially renamed the Captain

Emil J. Kapaun Post Office Building, in honor of the Kansan priest-hero. Unofficially, it's known as the "Good Thief Post Office."

A farmer's son, Emil J. Kapaun (1916–1951) was born in nearby Pilsen, Kansas, and ordained a priest for the Diocese of Wichita in 1940. Kapaun served as US Army chaplain during World War II and then the Korean War. He was known for praying with troops in foxholes and for offering Mass on the battlefield on the hood of a Jeep as a makeshift altar. Once, his tobacco pipe was shot out of his mouth by an enemy sniper.

On November 2, 1950, during the Battle of Unsan in North Korea, the chaplain and fellow comrades were captured and marched to a prison camp at Pyoktong. Invoking the aid of Saint Dismas, the Good Thief crucified next to Jesus, Kapaun regularly raided the enemy's larder for foodstuff and medicine for his starving and dying countrymen.

The Good Thief of Kansas died in the Pyoktong camp on May 23, 1951. He was thirty-five years old. Seventy years later, in 2021, his remains were identified, brought home to Kansas, and reinterred in a marble tomb in the east transept of the Cathedral of the Immaculate Conception in Wichita, Kansas. Declared Venerable in 2025, Kapaun is the only American on the road to sainthood with a namesake post office — the "Good Thief Post Office" at that.

Extreme Trivia
QUESTION 13

Remember the Alamo — but remember it began as a Spanish colonial mission. When was the mission founded? What was its original name?

First American Nun

On July 27, 1694, Lydia Longley's Puritan world changed forever. Abenaki Indians, French allies in the war against the English colonies, ambushed the William Longley farmstead near Groton, Massachusetts. Within minutes, her father, stepmother, and five siblings were dead. Lydia, twenty years old, and her younger siblings Betty and John were taken captive and forced to make the long journey north to French Canada by foot. Betty perished on the way, and John lived several years among the Abenaki before being freed by relatives in New England.

Lydia was taken to Montreal and ransomed, it's said, by Jacques Le Ber, a wealthy French Catholic widower who used his fortune to buy people's freedom. Lydia lived in the Le Ber home and was tutored in the French language. The young Puritan woman couldn't help but absorb the Catholic Faith in Catholic Montreal — everything, it seemed, was named for a saint. The Le Ber family even lived on Rue Saint-Paul (Saint Paul Street).

Around this time, Le Ber's daughter Jeanne, a noted recluse, entered the Congregation de Notre-Dame in Montreal. Shortly thereafter, Lydia abjured her Puritan religion and was baptized a Catholic on April 24, 1696, and christened Lydia-Madeleine. She followed Jeanne's example and joined the Notre-Dame nuns. Lydia Longley, or Sister Sainte-Madeleine as she was called, died in 1758 at age eighty-four, after sixty-one years as a religious sister.

On a boulder near the old Longley farmstead at Groton, an inscription recalls the 1694 massacre of the Longley family and the abduction of Lydia and her two siblings. What it doesn't say is that Lydia Longley, a Puritan by birth, was the first American-born woman to become a Catholic nun.

"What God Gives"

The life of Father Leon Gutowski made a complete loop — from

Poland to Wisconsin and then back to Poland. Born in 1896, Gutowski immigrated to America in 1912, at age sixteen. In 1927, the polyglot was ordained a priest for the Diocese of Superior, Wisconsin, and served rural ethnic parishes. Then, in a fascinating turn of events, Gutowski felt God calling him to return to his native Poland.

"Now after many years of prayer and meditation, I am convinced that I have that 'calling' from God to return to Poland," he wrote Superior's Bishop Theodore H. Reverman in 1936. Shortly thereafter, he did just that.

On June 12, 1941, Gutowski was leading a Corpus Christi procession at St. Lawrence Church in Zaręby, Poland, about sixty miles northeast of Warsaw, when Nazi troops took notice of the priest. He was arrested five days later. On August 29, he arrived at Dachau Concentration Camp, where he became prisoner 27112. When fellow prisoners complained about the squalid conditions of the camp, Gutowski was known to say, "*Co Bóg da, to bedzie*" ("What God gives, it will be"). A year later, on August 10, 1942, the forty-six-year-old priest was transported to Hartheim Castle, a killing center, in Hartheim, Austria, and executed in a gas chamber.

Gutowski's remarkable story might never have come to light had it not been for a tiny asterisk. While a seminarian in 2017, Father Dan Tracy of the Diocese of Superior decided to research the necrology of priests in his diocese. The line for Gutowski read, "Leon Gutowski, May 3, 1938*." (It's thought this date represents Gutowski's excardination from the Diocese of Superior.) At the bottom of the page, another asterisk read, "Date of death is unclear, letter on file said he died in a concentration camp."

Curious, Tracy began researching Gutowski's life. What God wills, will be. Not only did Tracy's research help Gutowski's American relatives discover what had happened to their ancestor, but Catholic America can now add another great man to its litany of holy men and women. Gutowski — born in Poland, ordained in America, and exterminated in Austria — followed the Lord, even unto death.

First American-Born Martyr

The farmer's son could plow a furrow as straight as an arrow but failed his first year of seminary theology. He struggled with learning Latin but mastered Spanish and Tz'utujil, an indigenous Mayan tongue, even translating the New Testament into Tz'utujil. He was Father Stanley Francis Rother, the first American-born priest and martyr to be beatified.

Born March 27, 1935, at Okarche, Oklahoma, the small-town farm boy was ordained in 1963 for the Diocese (now Archdiocese) of Oklahoma City. Five years later, Rother asked to be assigned to the diocesan mission in Santiago Atitlán, Guatemala. The farmer-priest plowed fields with his flock, fixed machinery, built an irrigation system, and founded a small hospital.

During this time, a violent civil war was raging in Guatemala between the militarist government forces and the guerillas. Rother tramped the roads looking for bodies of the *desaparecidos* — catechists and parishioners who had gone missing — to give them a Christian burial. Before long, his name appeared on a list of people to be executed. In a 1980 Christmas letter, Rother wrote his now-famous words, "The shepherd cannot run at the first sign of danger."

On July 28, 1981, Rother, forty-six years old, was murdered in his Guatemalan rectory, martyred for the Gospel. At the request of his flock, Rother's heart and spilled blood were interred under his mission church at Santiago Atitlán. His body was returned to his home state and now rests in the Blessed Stanley Rother Shrine in Oklahoma City. The farmer from Okarche was beatified in 2017, his two surviving siblings witnessing the historic event.

A Passion for the Passion

When Josef Meier (1904–1999) walked on stage in his white robe at the Black Hills Passion Play in Spearfish, South Dakota, he seemed to transcend life. And no wonder. For more than 9,000 performances, the German Catholic immigrant portrayed the Christus (German for Christ). If that didn't set a record, the three-block-long stage did. The play's backstory was even longer.

Originally called the Lünen Passion Play, the liturgical drama, which depicted the seven last days in the life of Christ, began in 1242 at the Cappenberg monastery in Lünen, Germany. (The famous Oberammergau Passion Play made its debut nearly four centuries later, in 1634.) Monks initially played the various roles, but eventually the script passed into the hands of Meier's ancestors. Josef became the seventh generation in his family to act in the play. In 1932, as Hitler and the Nazi Party were rising to power, Meier decided to bring the 700-year-old passion play to America.

While touring the country with the play, Meier visited Spearfish, a small town on the northern fringe of the Black Hills, in 1937. Here, Meier found the perfect setting for the outdoor drama: a natural amphitheater with superb acoustics and Lookout Mountain as a backdrop. Building sets forty to sixty feet tall went up, and seats were installed for 6,000 spectators. In Old World tradition, local residents played the 150 extras in the mob scenes. More than one minister became a thief and was crucified next to Jesus.

Season after season, Meier rode a donkey into Jerusalem. He gathered with his actor-disciples at the Last Supper and dragged a 150-pound cross up Calvary Hill, a real hill, and fell three times, just like his Savior. Nature sometimes added theatrical effects, including lightning during the crucifixion scene.

In 1991, Josef and his American wife, Clare, who portrayed Mother Mary in over 7,000 performances, passed the play's mantle to daughter Johanna and her husband, Guido Della Vecchia, both renowned opera singers. The couple had no children, and when they retired at the end of the 2008 season, the play retired with them. Still remembered by tens of thousands of Catholic pilgrims, the Black Hills Passion Play remains one of the longest-running professional passion plays in the nation.

American Conversion Story

The saga of Old St. Mary Church at Claremont, New Hampshire, is like no other conversion story in American history. Not only was it founded by an Episcopal-turned-Jesuit priest, but Father Virgil Barber's entire family — his wife and five children — all entered religious life!

Virgil Horace Barber was born May 9, 1782, at Claremont, the son of Daniel Barber, a Congregational Dissenter who quit the Puritanic sect and became an Episcopal priest. In 1807, Virgil — like father, like son — was ordained an Episcopal priest. He then married Jerusha Booth. One day, Virgil happened upon a novena booklet to St. Francis Xavier that belonged to an Irish servant-girl in his home. "His parallel cannot be found in the whole Protestant church," Virgil told Jerusha. Thus began an incredible work of grace.

During the winter of 1816–17, Virgil, Jerusha, and their children were received into the Catholic Church. A few months later, Virgil and Jerusha agreed to separate and enter religious life: Virgil joined the Society of Jesus and Jerusha the Visitation Order, taking the name of Sister Mary Augustine. (Their children would follow in their footsteps. Samuel became a Jesuit priest; Mary, Abigail, and Susan, Ursuline sisters; and Josephine, a Visitation sister, like her mother.)

On December 3, 1822, feast of St. Francis Xavier, Virgil was ordained a Jesuit priest at Boston, Massachusetts. He was then assigned to his hometown of Claremont to plant the first Catholic church in New Hampshire — "the land," Jesuit annals observed, "which had exacted a penalty of forty shillings an hour from anyone who harbored a Jesuit."

Erected in 1823 in Federal style, Old St. Mary Church has a peculiar look for a Catholic house of God. Tall and skinny, it measures twenty feet by forty-eight feet and fits forty people. The upper level of the two-story brick church served as a boys' school, the first Catholic school for boys in New England. The bottom level held the worship space. Daniel Barber, who left his Episcopal post in 1818 and — like son, like father — embraced the Catholic Faith, served at his son's Masses. Virgil died in 1847, twenty-four years a Catholic priest.

In 1870, a new St. Mary Church was built in the central part of town. Both churches (Old St. Mary is now considered part of West Claremont) are used to this day.

Extreme Trivia
QUESTION 14

If you're a bride and want to walk the country's longest aisle on your wedding day, what cathedral are you getting married in?

World's Wealthiest Nun

Her income was $1,000 a day, and she spent $1,000 a day. She hobnobbed with presidents and business tycoons. But you'd never know it by looking at her: She wore no jewels or fancy dresses. She was heiress Mother Katharine Drexel, called the Wealthiest Nun in the World.

Born in 1858, Katharine was the daughter of Francis A. Drexel, a fabulously wealthy investment banker in Philadelphia, Pennsylvania. Upon her father's death in 1885, Katharine and her two sisters inherited the income produced by $14 million — about $1,000 per day for each sister. (In today's dollars, the Drexel fortune would be worth an estimated $450 million. Some financial projections put the daily interest income at $63,000, or $23 million annually.)

But money didn't satisfy Katharine's soul. During trips out West in the 1880s, she saw the plight and poverty of Native Americans pushed onto reservations. In 1891, the thirty-two-year-old heiress founded the Sisters of the Blessed Sacrament and dedicated herself to serving the Indian and black minorities. Blazing a trail across the US, she established scores of missions, fifty schools for blacks, and twelve schools for native children. She also founded Xavier University of Louisiana, in New Orleans, the only historically black Catholic college or university in the nation.

Not surprisingly, Mother's work in the South infuriated the Ku Klux Klan. One day in the 1920s, the KKK threatened to tar and feather the pastor of Mother's school in Beaumont, Texas, and blow up his church. The sisters did what sisters do best: They prayed. As the story goes, a tornado dropped out of the sky, destroying the Klan's headquarters and killing two Klansmen. The KKK never messed with Mother again.

Mother Katharine Drexel died in 1955 at age ninety-six and was canonized in 2000. Splitting saintly hairs, some claim that Mother is the first American-born citizen to be canonized. (Canonized in 1975, St. Elizabeth Ann Seton was born in 1774 as a subject of King George III.) The mortal remains of the world's wealthiest nun-saint are entombed in the Cathedral Basilica of Saints Peter and Paul in Philadelphia, near the Drexel Family Altar.

The Great Prayer

Historic St. Mary's Mission in Stevensville, Montana, is a saga of extraordinarily great perseverance. In 1823–24, twelve Iroquois

Indians of Canada, fur trappers with Hudson's Bay Company of Ontario, were trapping in the region and decided to remain among the Salish Indians, also called the Flatheads. The Christianized Iroquois, in particular one named Big Ignace, began telling the Salish about the Black Robes — Jesuit missionaries who wore long black dresses like women, carried crucifixes, and prayed a Great Prayer.

Enthralled, the Salish and Nez Perce tribes dispatched four separate delegations to St. Louis, Missouri, to recruit Black Robes to come and teach them about God. In autumn 1831, the first delegation of Indians arrived in St. Louis, where two died and were buried in the old cathedral cemetery. But no Black Robes were available. Four years later, in 1835, Big Ignace and his two sons set out for St. Louis, where Black Robes baptized Big Ignace's sons, Charles and Francis Xavier. Again, no Black Robes could be spared to return with them to work among the Salish and Nez Perce.

Two years later, in 1837, Big Ignace led a third expedition. All five were massacred en route to St. Louis. Amazingly, the seekers didn't lose heart. In 1839, they sent a fourth delegation. This time they met with success. On September 24, 1841, ten years after the first delegation was sent to St. Louis, Jesuit legend Father Pierre-Jean De Smet arrived in Montana's Bitterroot Valley. As the Salish and Nez Perce watched with wide eyes and open hearts, De Smet offered up the Great Prayer: the Holy Sacrifice of the Mass.

Lighting Up the World

When the Great Depression swept across America in the 1930s, Father Frederick Bormann, pastor of Holy Cross Catholic Church in Ipswich, South Dakota, didn't curse the darkness. Too poor to buy candles for his church altar, Bormann begged or bought candle stubs from other churches and began making his own candles. He melted the stubs in stone crocks and poured the beeswax into molds. Wicks were made of plain string. In Depression jargon, it was called "making do."

Soon, Bormann was receiving orders for candles from priests in neighboring towns, and in 1933 the Lux Candle Company (Lux is Latin for "light") was born. Candle sales produced enough income to keep the Ipswich parish school open and pay down the parish debt. When the growing enterprise became too much for Bormann alone, he hired Joseph Heinz to help in the "candle factory," a little shed behind the rectory.

Bormann wasn't content, however. He wanted a 100 percent beeswax candle that would burn for at least forty hours and wouldn't wilt or topple over in the searing summer heat. He invented a little glass chimney, or "follower," that fit over the candle and slid down as the candle burned. The follower held the melted wax in a pool atop the candle, so the candle burned more slowly and without dripping. But there was still the problem of finding the right sized wick.

The candlemaker and his assistant set up a "forty-hour candle lab" in the Heinz's family bathtub (much to Mrs. Heinz's annoyance, it's said). Heinz would get out of bed periodically during the night to see how the candles were burning. Eventually, a candle burned for forty hours without flickering out, and the Lux Candle went on to light up altars around the world, including Rome. Lux Candles are still made today according to Bormann's specifications, with glass followers.

Mother of Firsts

Mother Elizabeth Ann Seton (1774–1821) was a "mother of firsts." In 1809, she founded the Sisters of Charity of St. Joseph at Emmitsburg, Maryland, the first American congregation of women religious. A year later, she began an academy for girls at Emmitsburg, one of the first free Catholic schools in the nation.

In 1975, she became the first native-born citizen to be canonized a saint — a sainted mother at that.

While we honor her with a "litany of firsts," Mother Seton knew sorrow in life. Her husband, William Seton, died of tuberculosis in 1803, leaving her a young widow at age twenty-nine. Two of her five children predeceased her. Once wealthy, she fell into poverty. When the Episcopal widow converted to Catholicism in 1805, she was shunned by New York's society elite. But Mother persevered and now ranks among America's greatest Catholic women. The liturgical calendars of both the Roman Catholic and Episcopal churches honor her on January 4, the date of her death. Mother's legacy is preserved at the National Shrine of Saint Elizabeth Ann Seton in Emmitsburg, where her remains rest inside her namesake basilica.

World's First Order of Black Nuns

In a spiritual Olympics, Venerable Mary Lange (c. 1794–1882) would win a gold medal for jumping hurdles. When the Caribbean native arrived in Baltimore, Maryland, around 1813, she had five seemingly impossible hurdles before her: She was a woman, she was a free person of color in a slave state, she was a Catholic in a mostly Protestant city, she spoke French, and she wanted to live large for the Lord. She cleared every hurdle, and then some.

Born Elizabeth Clarisse Lange in a French-speaking section of Santiago, Cuba, the bold, young trailblazer defied Maryland's slavery laws and began educating black girls in her home. In 1828, she began Saint Frances School for Colored Girls (now Saint Frances Academy), the oldest continuously operating Catholic school for African Americans in the country. In 1829 — thirty-four years before the Emancipation Proclamation — Elizabeth founded the Oblate Sisters of Providence, the world's first order of black nuns. Elizabeth took the religious name of Mary and became Mother Mary Lange.

Stained glass windows in Our Lady of Mount Providence Convent in Baltimore tell the order's story, including one window that depicts Mother with several of her quotes that guided her life. "Hasten to the Blessed Sacrament," one advises, and "Do all you can for the glory and honor of God."

Wonder Woman

She was born April 20, 1923, in Canton, Ohio, and baptized Rita Antoinette. At age nineteen, Rita was miraculously healed of a terrible stomach ailment. Two years later, Rita stole away from home and joined a monastery. One day while polishing the monastery floors with an electric scrubber, the thirty-something nun slipped and seriously injured her back. The night before back surgery, afraid she might become paralyzed or even die, the intrepid nun bargained with God. "If you let me walk again," she vowed, "I will build you a monastery in the South."

The nun was inspired to found a new religious community and became its abbess in 1960. One of the first women to join the fledging order was the nun's own mother, who became her religious daughter. To support themselves, the little band of sisters made and sold St. Peter's Fishing Lures. In 1961, the sisters left the Midwest for Alabama (can't get more Southern than that) to begin the nun's avowed monastery.

In 1978, while visiting a Baptist-run television station in Chicago, the nun boldly declared, "I gotta have one of these!" She converted the monastery garage into a TV studio and on August 15, 1981, launched the Eternal Word Television Network (EWTN) at Irondale, Alabama — now the largest religious television empire the world over. She sparred at times with liberal American bishops but found a staunch ally in Pope St. John Paul II. "Strong woman, courageous woman, charismatic woman," he called her.

Who was this Wonder Woman?

Mother Mary Angelica of the Annunciation, better known

as simply Mother Angelica. It was no coincidence that Annunciation was part of her religious name: Mother would announce the Gospel to the world. The Catholic media entrepreneur died Easter Sunday, March 27, 2016, a month shy of her ninety-third birthday. The lures she sold are still reeling in fish from around the world.

Stagecoach Mary

Black Mary had the temperament of a grizzly bear. She could cuss like a man, and she dressed like one. She wore a .38 Smith & Wes-

son under her apron and carried a rifle, just in case anyone got any ideas. Not that they would: Mary stood six feet tall and weighed over 200 pounds. Mary is an unruly character in American Catholic history, a reputation she would have loved. She's also a fine example that God's incredible people come in all shapes and sizes — and dispositions.

Black Mary's real name was Mary Fields. She was born a slave somewhere in Tennessee around 1832 and remained a slave for thirty-three years. After the Civil War, Mary, a Catholic, made her way North and wound up at an Ursuline convent in Toledo, Ohio, where she worked as a groundskeeper. When asked how things were going, she would reply, "I could use a cigar and a drink." Despite her shocking speech and unconventional ways, Mary found a friend in Mother Amadeus Dunne, the convent superior. It was a friendship made in heaven. (Some accounts claim that Black Mary had been a Dunne family slave and was Mother's personal maid before the nun took the veil. In any event, the two had a deep bond and love for the other.)

In 1884, Mother Amadeus was sent to Montana Territory to open a boarding school for girls at St. Peter's Mission, northwest of Cascade. When Black Mary got wind that Mother was deathly ill with pneumonia, she rushed to Montana to nurse her best friend back to health. Mary stayed to help Mother and became the mission forewoman. She fetched supplies, hauled freight, tended chickens, worked the laundry, and repaired buildings. But when Mary and a male worker at the mission got into a spat and drew guns on each other, the bishop sent her packing.

Mary didn't go far. Mother set her up in an eatery in Cascade. It's said that big-hearted Mary went broke twice; she was too quick to extend Christian charity and credit to people down on their luck. Mother then helped Mary land a star route contract with the United States Post Office between Cascade and St. Peter's Mission, making Mary the first black female mail carrier in American history. The route was thirty-four miles round trip, and Mary never missed a day in eight years (1895–1903). Guns always at the ready, Stagecoach Mary fended off wolves, bandits, and thieves. When the snow got too deep to use her mail wagon, she delivered the mail by snowshoe.

For all her gruffness and outsized reputation, Mary had a spiritual side. When Mass was held in Wedsworth Hall, before a Catholic church sprang up in Cascade, she took care of the altar. Once, she wore a beautiful dress with a long white veil and sat in the front pew at St. Peter's Mission Church with Mother. If jaws dropped, the angels stopped in mid-flight. Everyone in western Montana could recite the tales of Black Mary, even Catholic convert and actor Gary Cooper, who remembered seeing her when he was just a little shaver.

Black Mary died December 5, 1914, around the age of eighty-two. Her funeral was one of Cascade's largest, her coffin swallowed up in floral tributes. Townsfolk raised enough money to see her buried in Hillside Cemetery, overlooking the road to the old mission. She remains one of Montana's tallest legends, in more ways than one.

Extreme Trivia
QUESTION 15

In 1597, a baptized Guale Indian on St. Catherines Island, south of Savannah, Georgia, wanted to take a second wife. When Father Pedro de Corpa refused, he and four other Franciscan friars were killed. What is the collective name of these five Venerable Franciscans?

Prince of a Priest

Prince Demetrius Augustine Gallitzin had the world in his lap.

Born in 1770 to Russian royalty and baptized in the Russian Orthodox Church (Catherine the Great was his godmother), he forsook it all when he converted to Roman Catholicism at age sixteen. Under Russian law, the prince could no longer inherit his father's titles and estates or hold office in the Russian empire.

Up-and-coming aristocrats of the day were traditionally sent on grand tours of Europe to finish their education and introduce them to the world of high society. However, the French Revolution had broken out and Demitri's parents sent him to America instead. Rumor had it that his father hoped the American tour would squelch Demitri's desire to become a priest. It was not to be.

In 1792, Prince Demetrius took the pseudonym of Augustine Schmet, an abbreviation of his mother's maiden name Von Schmettau that became "Smith" in America, and boarded a ship for the New World — and a new life. The incognito prince entered St. Mary's Seminary in Baltimore, Maryland, and was ordained in 1795. "Father Smith" was the second priest ordained on American soil.

Called the Apostle of the Alleghenies, Smith traveled hill and dale of western Pennsylvania, ministering to scattered Catholics on the rugged frontier. In 1799, he erected a log cabin church — the forerunner of today's Basilica of St. Michael the Archangel — at Loretto. The Russian prince became a naturalized American citizen in 1802, under his assumed name of Augustine Smith. In 1809, the Pennsylvania legislature granted citizen Smith the right to resume the use of his given name Demetrius Gallitzin. He was incognito no more.

Gallitzin's dark flashing eyes were trained on his flock. According to lore, whenever he noticed the slightest hint of a sheep's deviation from Catholic practices, the offender would get doused with an extra sprinkling of holy water at Sunday Mass. If that didn't straighten out the wayward sheep, Gallitzin's stare down would. Nobody could escape his soul-penetrating eyes — eyes that made grown men weep and repent on the spot.

America's prince-priest died a pauper in 1840 and was buried in an eight-dollar coffin. His mortal remains await the resurrection in a walk-in crypt just outside the basilica. The Russian prince, who had given up a kingdom on earth to inherit the kingdom of heaven, was declared a Servant of God in 2005.

Little Cajun Saint

Servant of God Charlene Richard (1947–1959) was your typical twelve-year-old. She loved Elvis Presley music and "sock hops," all the rage in the 1950s. One day in May 1959, after reading a book about St. Thérèse of Lisieux, Charlene Marie, the second of ten children, asked her grandmother if she might become a saint like the Little Flower. Her grandmother replied, "Yes, if you pray like her."

Nobody knows what the tweenager prayed, but a couple of months later she was diagnosed with acute lymphatic leukemia and hospitalized at Our Lady of Lourdes Hospital in Lafayette, Louisiana. When Father Joseph F. Brennan, hospital chaplain, broke the news to Charlene that she was going to die, he suggested that she offer up her pain for the conversion of souls and the healing of the sick. On Brennan's daily rounds,

Charlene would ask, "Who are we praying for today?" (It was later claimed that every person Charlene prayed for while on her deathbed was either healed or became Catholic.)

Two weeks after being diagnosed, Charlene died on August 11, 1959. Almost immediately, pilgrims began visiting her grave at St. Edward Catholic Church Cemetery at Church Point, Louisiana, asking for her pious intercession. Reports of favors received began pouring in. Over the years, Charlene has earned a reputation of being especially responsive to prayer requests from priests.

Called the Little Cajun Saint, Charlene — Louisiana's very own Little Flower — is the youngest American up for sainthood.

Section Four

INCREDIBLE TRIVIA

How many Catholic cathedrals and parish churches are blessed with incredible trivia? They all are! There isn't one church without a curious story or two. The trivia pieces in this section don't clamor for greatness or a place in the record books. They just are, in a serendipitous sort of way. Plucked from parish histories or diocesan archives, the stories run the gamut — from JFK's church pew, to mysteries worthy of Sherlock Holmes, to "holy oil" in Alaska.

You'll also hear tales of bishops, all anointed with good humor, and even a few miracle stories. So, curl up with a thick slice of "Catholic Cheese" (invented by Spanish Franciscans) and binge read your way across Catholic America.

Presidential Pew

When Massachusetts Senator John F. Kennedy and Jacqueline Lee Bouvier were married on September 12, 1953, at Saint Mary, Our Lady of the Isle Roman Catholic Church in Newport, Rhode

Island, it was the wedding of the decade. Later, as President and First Lady of the United States, they spent weekends in Newport and worshiped at Saint Mary's, always sitting in pew number ten. Kennedy wasn't the first president to have been married by a Catholic priest, however.

On February 10, 1899, Father Ramon Mestres married Herbert C. Hoover, a Quaker, and Lou Henry, an Episcopalian, at her parents' home in Monterey, California. The couple originally wanted Doctor William Thoburn, a Methodist minister and a professor at Stanford University, their alma mater, to officiate. But he died just weeks before the wedding, so they asked Mestres, a family friend, to perform the civil ceremony. Interestingly, Hoover, who was elected president in 1928, ran against Alfred E. Smith, the first Catholic nominated for president of the US.

Blazing Saddle

Historic St. Joan of Arc Roman Catholic Church in Las Vegas, Nevada, began with a "blazing saddle." Bishop Lawrence Scanlan of Salt Lake City — the diocese overseeing Las Vegas at the time — was riding a horse through the desert town one hot July day. It was so blistering hot that the bishop felt like he was being burned alive like Joan of Arc. In 1908, Scanlan named the first parish in Las Vegas for Joan. He didn't care that Joan hadn't yet been canonized (she would be in 1920). She was burned at the stake and he in his blazing saddle.

Wedding of the Sea

The Wedding of the Sea at Catholic churches up and down the Atlantic Seaboard is one of the most unique weddings ever. It doesn't unite a man and a woman but the sea and a town. Tradition holds the centuries-old custom originated at Venice, Italy, when an archbishop got caught in a tempest at sea. He threw his episcopal ring into the water and begged God to save both him and the coastal city.

On August 15 — Solemnity of the Assumption of the Blessed Virgin Mary — parishioners at Our Lady Star of the Sea Church in Cape May, New Jersey (and other parishes along the Atlantic coast), process from the church to the ocean with a statue of Mary. A priest offers prayers, imploring God to bless both the ocean and the town. The priest is then rowed out into the ocean where he places a "ring" — a wreath of flowers — upon the water, symbolizing the wedding of the town and the sea.

Case of the Missing Cornerstone(s)

Calling Sherlock Holmes — and maybe Catholic sleuths Father Brown and Father Dowling too. The cornerstone of St. James Cathedral in Seattle is missing! You can search high and low in the Italian Renaissance-style edifice, inside and out, and no cornerstone is to be found. But Bishop Edward J. O'Dea laid the cornerstone for the new cathedral on November 12, 1905. Some 5,000 spectators, including the press, witnessed the grand event. The Archdiocese of Seattle even holds the silver trowel that O'Dea used in the ceremony. But where, oh where, is that blessed cornerstone?

\+ + + + +

And where, pray tell, is the cornerstone of St. Patrick's Cathedral in New York City? Archbishop John J. Hughes ritually blessed the stone on Sunday, August 15, 1858, but left the stone open for people to leave offerings. It was sealed two years later to the day, on August 15, 1860. And here the trail goes stone cold. Where exactly was the cornerstone laid? When did it go missing? Did the feisty archbishop place the stone inside a wall for all eternity, never to be seen again? The 165-year-old puzzle continues to this day.

Three Times a Miracle

Can a miracle strike three times in the same place? Believe it or not, it happened at Coral Miracle Church at Keanae, on the Hawaiian island of Maui. In 1860, testified an eyewitness priest, native Hawaiians decided to build a new church to replace a shack they had been using for Mass. While rocks abounded in the area, the sand and the coral — needed to make the mortar — would have to come from the sea. But diving for coral in deep water was

arduous and dangerous. Prayers went up for the divers' safety.

On the appointed day of the dive, a fierce storm began to rage and washed heaps of coral ashore. It was a miracle, everyone said. When it was discovered more coral would be needed to plaster the church's thick walls, another storm coughed up more coral from the sea — miracle number two. With no beach in the area, the divers still had to bring up sand. Incredibly, in a third miraculous event, monster waves swept the unneeded coral back to sea and left behind a huge mound of white sand!

Tornado Forecast

When Germans from Russia founded the small Catholic town of Liebenthal, Kansas, and St. Joseph's Church in the mid-1870s, they reportedly had insider knowledge: the weather intel of Native Americans. Because of its unique geography, the area was said to be tornado proof.

Settlers had good reason to be worried about tornadoes. The town of Codell, Kansas, was hit by twisters in three consecutive years, 1916 (F2), 1917 (F3), and 1918 (F4), each year on the same date — May 20. So far, no tornado has touched Liebenthal or St. Joseph's Church, just as native intelligence foretold.

Happy New Year?

Why do some Catholics living in Old Colonial America wish each other "Happy New Year" on March 25? Because they're looking back in time and following a centuries-old tradition. Until 1752, England and colonial America followed the astronomically incorrect Julian calendar, which had, over the centuries, fallen behind by eleven days, and not the more accurate Gregorian calendar instituted by Pope Gregory XIII in 1582. The first day of the Julian new year was March 25 and aptly coincided with the feast of the Annunciation, when the Archangel Gabriel announced to Mary that she would give birth to the Messiah. The last day of the Julian calendar year was March 24, New Year's Eve.

England and colonial America adopted the Gregorian calendar in 1752. Under the old calendar, December 31, 1750, was followed by January 1, 1750. (December was the tenth month and January the eleventh.) Under the Calendar (New Style) Act 1750, New Year's Day was moved to January 1, starting with the first January 1 after December 31, 1751. Thus, in England and colonial America, 1751 was a short year of just over nine months, running from March 25, 1751, until December 31, 1751. Then, in order to bring the dates in line with Western Europe, most of which had adopted the Gregorian calendar by 1700, eleven days needed to be dropped. So the colonists (and their English cousins) went to bed on September 2, 1752, and woke up on September 14!

The calendar switch went off without a hitch, except maybe for grumpy saints whose feast days fell between September 3 and September 13. Calendar makeover or not, the feast of the Annunciation each year celebrates the dawning of a new spiritual era for humankind. And who wouldn't say Happy New Year to that?

Strangest Chapel

The Father Weikamp Chapel in Cross Village, Michigan, may be the strangest chapel in America. In the mid-1800s, one story goes, Father Johannes B. Weikamp, TOR, dug himself a grave and built a mausoleum chapel over it. The portly Franciscan would visit the mausoleum daily and spend time meditating, presumably upon death. Then, Weikamp made himself a wooden coffin and kept it at the foot of his bed. The coffin was the last thing he saw at night and the first thing in the morning.

Death came for Weikamp in 1889, when he was accidentally dragged by his horse. The seventy-year-old was laid out in his coffin and buried in his mausoleum chapel, in what is now the Father Weikamp Cemetery. Apparently, Weikamp didn't dig a very deep grave because one day villagers noticed a crack in the coffin lid. They exhumed the wooden box and discovered the priest was practicing the Franciscan charism of loving God's creatures, even in death. Squirrels were using his coffin to store nuts!

Gone-with-the-Wind Bishop

When Margaret Mitchell's blockbuster novel *Gone with the Wind* was released in 1936, Catholic readers in Georgia took notice. The novel, set in Georgia during the Civil War and Reconstruction era, included a character named Gerald O'Hara, the hard-drinking Irish father of Scarlett O'Hara, the protagonist. Mitchell reportedly checked reams of old records to make sure that none of her fictional names were real, but she apparently missed the appointment of Bishop Gerald P. O'Hara to the Diocese of Savannah in 1935. And that's how the good-looking bishop — as handsome as Rhett Butler, many claimed — came to be "gone with the wind."

Skyway Church

Not rain or snow, not even the scorching summer sun, can keep workers from attending noon Mass at St. Olaf Catholic Church in downtown Minneapolis, Minnesota. The mid-1950s church of contemporary design is connected to a major skyway system — a second-story, enclosed walkway with bridges that connect one building to another. Workers just follow the streets in the sky to St. Olaf's and Jesus, Our Lord.

St. Joske's

Looking for St. Joske's Church in downtown San Antonio, Texas? Try the American spelling: St. Joseph's. Founded in 1868, St. Joseph's is famous for its German stubbornness. In the 1940s, Joske's Department Store wanted to expand its downtown location and offered to buy the neo-Gothic church and church grounds. Parishioners at St. Joseph's unanimously said, "No way, Joske!" And so, Joske's built around three sides of St. Joseph's, thus the moniker "St. Joske's." Joske's is no more, but St. Joseph's still stands — the "Jewel in the Heart of San Antonio."

Extreme Trivia QUESTION 16

I am the granddaughter of a slave and accomplished something no other American can claim. In 1989, I spoke before a meeting of US Catholic bishops and got them to stand, link hands, and join me in singing "We Shall Overcome." Some say that was my first miracle. I was declared a Servant of God in 2018. Who am I?

The Missing Mystery

There were fifteen mysteries of the Rosary when St. Patrick Church in Nashua, New Hampshire, was built in the early 1900s — and therein lies a mystery. Why do the stained glass windows in this gorgeous house of God depict only fourteen mysteries? The answer is invisible. The Third Glorious Mystery, the Descent of the Holy Spirit, isn't really missing at all. During the Eucharistic Prayer at Mass, the priest asks the Holy Spirit to descend upon the bread and wine so they may become the body and blood of Christ.

The Third Glorious Mystery is here — in Spirit.

22,000 Miles to Ordination

What a pity Bishop François N. Blanchet couldn't collect frequent traveler miles. He surely set a world record for traveling the most miles for episcopal consecration. In November 1844, the French

Canadian missionary, laboring in the vast Oregon Country, received a letter from the Vatican addressed to the "bishop elect." Since there weren't any bishops in the West to consecrate him, Blanchet headed for Montreal, Canada, where he had been ordained a priest twenty-five years earlier.

In early December 1844, Blanchet boarded a ship in Oregon, touched at Honolulu, Hawaii, rounded Cape Horn, and landed in England. He boarded another vessel for Boston, Massachusetts, and then journeyed by rail to Canada. By the time Blanchet arrived in Montreal in late June 1845, he had logged an epic 22,000 miles! He was consecrated bishop on July 25 in Montreal's St. James Cathedral.

And then began the long journey home.

Dedication Blooper

Immaculate Conception Catholic Church in Steilacoom, Washington — the state's oldest standing Catholic church — was dedicated to the wrong saint. Originally called St. Michael the Archangel, the church was built twice from the same lumber. The first time was in 1855 by soldiers at Fort Steilacoom. In 1864, the frame church was dismantled, board by board, hauled by wagon to nearby Steilacoom, and raised a second time on a hill overlooking Puget Sound.

When Bishop Augustin-Magloire Blanchet, brother of world traveler Bishop François N. Blanchet, dedicated the newly rebuilt church, he inadvertently gave Saint Michael the boot and named it the Immaculate Conception. Or so the story goes.

Tower of Torture

It's not exactly the Tower of London, but getting to the top of the Scenic Tower at the Basilica and National Shrine of Mary Help of Christians at Holy Hill near Hubertus, Wisconsin, might feel a bit like torture. Annually, thousands of "martyrs" voluntarily huff and puff their way up 178 steps, in the tower's narrow winding staircase, to an observation deck in the nearly 200-foot-tall spire. If the climb doesn't take their breath away, the view of the Kettle Moraine countryside will.

Three Holy Peas in a Pod

What do a Sacred Hearts priest, a Franciscan nun, and a former drunk have in common? All three were born in different countries, all three tended to the Kalaupapa leper colony on the Hawaiian island of Molokai, and all three are venerated in the Catholic Church. Who are these three holy peas in a pod? St. Damien de Veuster of Belgium, St. Marianne Cope, a German immigrant, and Servant of God Joseph Dutton, a Civil War veteran born at Stowe, Vermont.

God Hears

In 1947, the legend runs, four priests from Denver, Colorado, were headed home after a summer vacation to Wyoming. They were traveling a lonely stretch of road between Gillette and Douglas. After an hour and a half on the "lonesome highway" — they had seen only two other cars — one priest remarked, "The bishop must have a heck of a time covering all this territory."

The words from the priest's lips must have flown directly to God's ears. On August 2, the priest, Father Hubert M. Newell, was named Coadjutor Bishop of the Diocese of Cheyenne. Four years later, Newell was made bishop. The lonesome diocese covers the entire state of Wyoming — 97,813 square miles, an area larger than the United Kingdom.

Latter-Day Cathedral

The Cathedral of the Madeleine in Salt Lake City, Utah, is the only cathedral in the country named for St. Mary Magdalene (Madeleine in French). Erected in the early 1900s, the Romanesque-Gothic cathedral probably has more artistic references to Madeleine than any church outside Europe.

A seventeenth-century Italian painting of the Madeleine adorns the reredos, while a mural of Madeleine washing the feet of Jesus graces the west transept. In the east transept, another mural portrays Madeleine and the Resurrected Jesus. Madeleine was the first person to see Jesus after he had risen from the dead.

But it's neither name nor painting that entices Latter Day Saints to visit the cathedral. Rather, they're drawn by the enormous sanctuary murals painted by Felix Lieftuchter in 1918. The right mural portrays Old Testament figures and the left mural various saints throughout the ages. It's said the artist used Mormons as models for his paintings, and their latter-day descendants come looking for their "Catholic ancestors."

Catholic Cheese

Who invented American Cheese? Spanish Franciscan friars in California, of course. Between 1769 and 1823, the gray-robed missionaries erected a string of twenty-one missions from San Diego to Sonoma, including Mission San Carlos Borroméo de Carmelo at Monterey. Because the missions needed to be self-sufficient (no takeout in those days), the friars brought fruit and vegetable seeds and cows from Europe. When there was a surplus of milk, the friars made a white cheese called *queso blanco país*, or country peasant cheese. The "Catholic Cheese" is known today as Monterey Jack and is America's original cheese.

Bullet-Hole Church

Every new bishop is curious about his new cathedral. When Bishop Claude M. Dubuis, CM, arrived at St. Mary's Cathedral in Galveston, Texas, during the Civil War in 1863, he needed an umbrella — inside the church. "The cathedral is riddled with bullets," he wrote. "Only on dry days can I say Mass within its walls." The historic Gothic cathedral (now a basilica) is also noted for a singular gift: 500,000 bricks shipped from Belgium as ballast.

With My People

Servant of God Patrick Ryan (1845–1878) was a priest on the go — before and after his death. In 1872, the young, handsome Irish native took charge of Sts. Peter and Paul Church in Chattanooga, Tennessee. When yellow fever struck the city in 1878, people lit for the hills to escape the scourge. Ryan stayed behind, tending to physical and spiritual needs of victims, succumbing to the plague himself. He was thirty-three years old.

The priest's last request: "Bury me in Chattanooga among my people." He was buried as he asked, in the church yard. In 1886, his remains were exhumed and escorted by a cortege of over 100 carriages to Mount Olivet Cemetery, the new Catholic cemetery in town. The hero rested there until 2021, when his casket was brought back to his parish church, now the Basilica of Sts. Peter and Paul, and re-entombed beneath the Fourteenth Station of the Cross (Jesus is laid in the tomb). The Martyr of Charity is here to stay, among his people.

Miracle at St. Casimir's

When St. Casimir Church in Cleveland, Ohio, closed after its "last Mass" on November 8, 2009, Our Lady went to work. Wasn't the Polish church now hers? Just days earlier, a Polish priest had dedicated the century-old Romanesque gem to the Blessed Mother. The night after the church closure, Our Lady appeared in a dream to parishioner Michael Klymiuk-Wieczerski and said, "Don't leave me." The retired doctor and others took that to mean the church.

The very next Sunday parishioners began a prayer vigil outside St. Casimir's locked doors. Sunday after Sunday, in bitter cold and blistering heat, they prayed in Polish and English, imploring Our Lady to work a miracle and reopen the historic church. They also made a formal appeal to the Vatican. How long would Mary's rebels stand?

On March 7, 2012, after nearly two and one-half years of prayer-protests, the Vatican issued a decree: Reopen the church! The miracle of St. Casimir's had come to pass.

Extreme Trivia
QUESTION 17

Why is a pair of dice depicted in ceiling artwork at the Cathedral of the Incarnation in Nashville, Tennessee?

"Wrong Way" Cemetery

When Judgment Day comes, residents of St. Joseph Cemetery at Rayne, Louisiana, will discover they're headed the wrong way. Instead of facing east like many traditional graveyards, the above-ground crypts are positioned north–south. The "Wrong Way" cemetery even earned a citation in *Ripley's Believe It or Not.*

The cemetery wasn't always in the wrong. When the railroad bypassed the town in the late 1800s, the town up and moved to be closer to the tracks. St. Joseph's Cemetery moved too. Somehow, the new burial plots were mislaid north–south. When the grave mistake was discovered, too many dead had already been reburied, so it was decided to let them be — headed the wrong way.

To Catch a Thief

On May 19, 1927, Our Lady's statue vanished from the Basilica and National Shrine of Our Lady of Consolation at Carey, Ohio. Kidnapped! A ransom letter was found tacked to the rectory door demanding $200 ($3,500 today) for her safe return. The snatcher telephoned the rector, Father Aloys Fish, OFM Conv, and stated his terms. He would send a messenger to collect the ransom money and divulge Our Lady's whereabouts if Fish promised not to follow the messenger. Fish agreed, and found the statue stowed in a nearby public restroom.

The snatcher made a fatal mistake, though. While making arrangements with a messenger to fetch the ransom money, he was overheard by the sheriff's son, who alerted his father. During the trial, the thief confessed to robbing some 7,000 churches! Our Lady had caught a serial thief.

Bread of Life

When the rural Colorado parishes of St. John, in Stoneham, and St. Joseph, in Akron, celebrated their centennial anniversaries — Stoneham in 2016 and Akron in 2018 — they gave back to God what God had given to them: wheat. The prayer "Blessed are you, Lord God of all creation, for through your goodness we have received the bread we offer you: fruit of the earth and work of human hands, it will become for us the bread of life" became profoundly real to the local wheat growers. The bread of life was made from the work of their very hands.

Likewise, the wine used at Mass at a third area parish, St. Mary's in Brush, is the work of human hands. A parishioner with a small vineyard makes and gives the wine to St. Mary's so it may become their spiritual drink.

Japanese "Book of Ruth"

The story of Father William Stoecke, SVD, echoes the Old Testament Book of Ruth. During World War II, the pastor of St. Francis Xavier Church in San Francisco, California, followed his people to a Japanese detention camp. On February 19, 1942, two months after Japan bombed Pearl Harbor in Hawaii, President

Franklin D. Roosevelt signed Executive Order No. 9066. People of Japanese descent had just days to dispose of their property and relocate to internment camps, where the "suspected spies" couldn't sabotage the war effort.

Stoecke, who had served eleven years as a missionary in Akita, Japan, joined his Japanese flock at Camp Topaz, a crudely built compound near Delta, Utah. The sixty-five-year-old German native sizzled alongside the internees in the summer heat and shivered with them in the winter cold. After the war, Stoecke helped his people resettle in San Francisco. Masses in Japanese are still conducted at St. Francis Xavier Church, built in 1939 as a Japanese national parish.

In 1994, the parish welcomed the Deaf Catholic community and is known today as St. Benedict Parish for the Deaf at St. Francis Xavier Church.

Dead and Gone

The Brothers of Saint Joseph in Oklahoma City, Oklahoma, had one of the most unique charisms in America: to bury the dead. Founded in 1960 by French Canadian Brother Joseph Levesque, the order planned, plotted, and were caretakers of a new burial ground in Oklahoma City, known today as Resurrection Memorial Cemetery. Levesque even designed the distinctive cemetery chapel. At its height, the pious association reported twenty-six followers.

The monks followed the Rule of Saint Benedict and wore a black habit. They observed the liturgy of the hours and attended daily Mass. When the winds of Vatican II began blowing through the order, radical reforms signaled the beginning of the end. The black habit fell by the wayside. Instead of professing vows, the brothers signed a one-year agreement. Vocations dried up. By the end of 1973, the order was dead to the world.

Bishop Who Refused to Pray

When Union forces occupied Natchez, Mississippi, in 1863, Bishop William H. Elder of the Diocese of Natchez deliberately disobeyed a Union order. (The Diocese of Natchez once served all of Mississippi until the state was divided into two dioceses, Jackson and Biloxi.) He refused to have his priests recite a public prayer at Sunday Mass for elected officials of the US government, including President Abraham Lincoln. Elder asserted the order violated Church prerogative and the US Constitution.

Elder was exiled from Natchez and held prisoner at Vidalia, Louisiana. Seventeen days later, he was released. It's said that Elder never did recite the Union prayer. He stuck to his guns and his religious principles.

"Coolest" Cathedral

When electricity first arrived in Cleveland, Ohio, and the summer weather got hot and sticky, the Cathedral of St. John the Evangelist turned on its "air conditioner." Large blocks of ice were hauled down into the church basement and fans positioned to blow air over the ice. The cooled air then cooled down the worship space upstairs. The 175-year-old Gothic cathedral claims to be the first air-conditioned church in the country.

Touchdown Jesus

Who stands 134 feet high, sixty-eight feet wide, and is seen by millions during televised football games at the University of Notre Dame in Notre Dame, Indiana? It's none other than Touchdown Jesus! Decorating the south exterior wall of Hesburgh Library, the country's tallest Jesus mural looms over the north end zone of Notre Dame Stadium. Jesus' arms are upraised just like a football referee when a touchdown is scored.

The mural wasn't intended to be a football metaphor. Officially titled *Word of Life* and unveiled in 1964, the library mural, constructed of some 6,700 individual pieces of granite, depicts a procession of Christian scholars and saints throughout the ages, with Christ the Teacher at the top. For the football team lagging behind on the scoreboard, however, the towering image becomes a prayer: "Touchdown, Jesus, touchdown!"

Defending the Church

Around 1910, the Ku Klux Klan decided to burn down the newly built St. Mary of the Knobs Catholic Church in Floyds Knobs, Indiana. But the Klan was no match for "Mary's men." Father Joseph Sermersheim, pastor, met the Klan at the bottom of the hill and nodded up toward the church. More than 100 guns were peeking out from behind tombstones and sticking out church windows. Seeing they were outnumbered, the Klansmen left. Unlike Mary's men, these cowards weren't about to risk their lives for their religious beliefs. The historic brick church, with fortresslike towers, still stands today.

Crossing the Line

St. Catherine Labouré Church in Copperhill, Tennessee, crosses the line — the Tennessee–Georgia state line. The front door of the church, dedicated in 1950, is located in extreme southeastern Tennessee and the altar sits in Georgia. Sermons delivered from the pulpit in Georgia are directed to the congregation sitting in Tennessee.

Even more confusing is St. Boniface Church in Jellico, Tennessee. The church sits on the Kentucky side of the state line, by a whisker. Directly behind the church is the Tennessee border. The mailing address is 76 West Sycamore, Williamsburg, Kentucky, where the pastor resides. But the street address is Catholic Avenue, Jellico, Tennessee. The street address is located in the Diocese of Knoxville, Tennessee, but the parish belongs to the Diocese of Lexington, Kentucky.

Miracle of the Sun

On November 19, 1971, the House of Mary Shrine at Yankton, South Dakota, witnessed its own miracle of the sun — not once but three times, as three giant crosses were raised on a bluff overlooking Lewis and Clark Lake. When the first fifty-foot-tall wooden cross was raised, a dazzling halo of light with the colors of a rainbow appeared around the sun, then faded away. As the second cross went up, another halo was spotted around the sun. And again, when the third cross was raised. A photo of the sun halos can be found inside the shrine's St. Joseph Chapel, as well as a stained glass window depicting the phenomenal event.

The FBI

Father Thomas Sheridan was the last of Wyoming's FBI — Foreign Born Irish. When he died in 2021, a legacy died too. For many decades, FBI clergy had a presence in the Diocese of Cheyenne. In fact, its first two bishops — Maurice F. Burke and Thomas M. Lenihan — were FBI. When Sheridan, born in County Cavan, Ireland, arrived in Wyoming in 1964, nearly half the diocesan clergy were Irish born. Three of them were Sheridan's cousins.

Coincidentally, Sheridan served at Holy Name Catholic Church in Sheridan, a town named for General Philip Sheridan (not FBI), said to be Father Sheridan's American relative. In remembrance of days gone by, a Celtic-style cross honoring Wyoming's FBI stands outside St. Patrick's Catholic Church in Casper.

Prophetic Sermon

On Sunday, November 21, 1897, Father Bernard J. Menge, pastor of Old St. Mary's in Cincinnati, Ohio, climbed up into the church's newly installed pulpit. His eyes passing over the German congregation, he preached a fine sermon on the Judgment. He never used the pulpit again. Two hours later, the sixty-six-year-old priest was found dead in a rectory chair. Judgment Day had come.

Extreme Trivia
QUESTION 18

I am the only Catholic missionary to have my portrait done in corn. Yes, corn! Who am I? And where can you see my one of a kind artwork?

Brighter Than Hell

Is there a hell? Yes, the *Catechism of the Catholic Church* (see CCC 1035) tells us so. But did you know Hell is also a town, and it's in Michigan? According to one yarn, the hamlet got its name in the 1830s when two German travelers got off the stagecoach on a sunny afternoon. One German said to the other, "So Schön hell" ("So beautifully bright"). The "hell" or bright part stuck. And yes, this Hell — near Ann Arbor in the southeastern region of the Mitten State — freezes over.

Southern Belle

She's 165-plus years old and reigns over Bay St. Louis, Mississippi, from an outdoor gazebo shrine with all the grace and charm of a southern belle. But Our Lady of the Woods isn't your typical Madonna. When Hurricane Katrina decimated the town in 2005 and swept the pews of Our Lady of the Gulf Catholic Church into the Gulf of Mexico, Our Lady didn't succumb to the elements. So, what is Mary's secret to long life? She's made of plaster of paris, a material not known to age well. The answer may be a devoted priest.

Father Stanislaus Buteux was returning from France in the late 1850s, when a violent tempest sheered the mast off his ship. The priest plunged to his knees and entreated the Blessed Mother to spare the vessel, promising to erect a shrine in her honor.

Our Lady of the Woods Shrine was dedicated shortly thereafter. The Lady and the Infant she holds both face the Mississippi Sound calm as can be — come hurricane or high water.

Oldest Immigrants

The Shrine of St. Martin of Tours in Louisville, Kentucky, was built in 1853 by hardworking German immigrants. On New Year's Eve 1901, two unlikely immigrants arrived at the antebellum church: the bones of Saints Magnus and Bonosa. They are by far the oldest (and most unique) immigrants in American history — and perhaps a love story at that.

According to tradition, Bonosa, a twenty-something virgin, was executed around AD 207 in Rome's Colosseum for her Christian beliefs. Some say Magnus, a Roman centurion, fell in love with Bonosa at first sight and jumped into the ring to save her. He was killed on the spot. The saintly skeletons, attired in regal robes and wearing crowns of martyrdom, repose in glass reliquaries under St. Martin's two side altars.

Twist on Faith

Goliad, Texas, is a twist on *faith.* In a peculiar reversal of church and state, the State of Texas owns a Catholic mission, and the Catholic Church (the Diocese of Victoria) owns a presidio (fort). But Presidio La Bahía, established in 1749, isn't any old stone fort: This is where the Texas Revolution began. On December 20, 1835, a contingent of ninety-two Texians, as they were called, signed the First Declaration of Texas Independence from Mexico in the presidio's Our Lady of Loreto Chapel.

One of the oldest active parishes in the country, Our Lady of Loreto Chapel has a few legends of its own. In 1946, the angel Gabriel appeared at the chapel in a Texas-size fresco of the Annunciation. Painted by Antonio Garcia, the "Michelangelo of South Texas," the angel Gabriel has six toes. When people asked the artist about the extra digit, he would reply, "Do you know how many toes an angel has?" Still others say the sixth toe is a shadow, fooling the eye.

Cat's Church

Can a church mouse find sanctuary at Old Mission San Juan Bautista in San Juan Bautista, California? Not for long. A "cat door," carved into the bottom of a wooden blue door in the Guadalupe Chapel, allows resident cats to enter the Spanish colonial church to do their ordained work.

The cat door was created in the 1800s because voracious mice were eating up the mission's harvest. The cats were so proficient in their holy calling that the mission got the reputation as the "Cat's Church."

By Hook or Crook

In 1974, Father Gregory Harding Keller appeared on *What's My Line?*, a TV quiz show on which a celebrity panel tried to guess the guest's occupation or claim to fame. Keller's "line": He invented a machine in 1957 that put the hook or crook in the candy cane. Before then, the canes were "hooked" or bent by hand as the candy sticks came off the assembly line, a labor-intensive process that resulted in a high breakage rate.

A priest with the Diocese of Little Rock, Arkansas, Keller designed the hooking machine — known as the Keller Machine — for Bobs Candies of Albany, Georgia, run by his brother-in-law Bob McCormack and family. The machine allowed the company, one of the world's leading candy cane producers, to mass-produce the red-and-white striped Christmas candy. And that's how the "J" came to be in the upside-down candy cane — Jesus, the reason for the season.

Escape by Piano

A priestly assignment to Merigold, Mississippi, in 1905 nearly cost Father Aloysius Heick, SVD, his life. When the German native tried to start a local school for black children, he was greeted with death threats. Not everyone shared his passion for educating all children. To avoid being lynched, lore has it, Heick was smuggled out of town in a piano case on a horse-drawn wagon. It may be the only piano escape in American Catholic history.

Threats didn't keep the zealous Divine Word Missionary out of the Magnolia State, however. Heick began St. Mary's Church in Vicksburg in 1906; Holy Ghost, Jackson, in 1909; St. Joseph, Meridian, in 1910; and Sacred Heart, Greenville, in 1913. Seven years later, Heick helped found Sacred Heart College at Greenville, the nation's first Catholic seminary for black men. Because of intimidation by the Ku Klux Klan, the seminary was moved in 1923 to Bay St. Louis, Mississippi, and renamed St. Augustine Seminary.

The seminary's first black priests were ordained in 1934.

Muskrat Fridays

Fish isn't the only aquatic protein that Downriver Catholics in southeast Michigan can eat on Lenten Fridays. There's also muskrat.

In the late 1790s, Father Gabriel Richard, PSS, witnessed French Canadian fur trappers and their families literally going hungry during Lent. Food stored up from the fall harvest was depleted, and ice-covered waterways made fishing difficult. Some starving families were eating hay for sustenance. Rationalizing muskrats lived in water like fish ("rats" can swim under water for up to twenty minutes), the French priest sought a dispensation from the Vatican for Downriver Catholics to eat the furry rodent on Lenten days of abstinence.

The dispensation is still in effect today. Instead of fish fries, some parishes hold a muskrat dinner. Bishop Kenneth J. Povish, Michigan born and former shepherd of the Diocese of Lansing, Michigan, once quipped, "Anybody that eats muskrat is doing an act of penance worthy of the greatest of saints." Maybe so, but for the starving fur trappers and families, "rats" were the food of life. (For inquiring culinary minds, muskrat does not taste just like chicken.)

Hats Off for the Lord

St. Lawrence Church in Stangelville, Wisconsin, has a thing about hats. Around 1863, six Czech men were watching three Irishmen chop down a large tree to make way for a road. The falling tree suddenly veered in the wrong direction and landed on the Czech men. The only casualty was a hat — the man wearing it was thankful it wasn't his head! Taking this as a miracle, the Czechs hastened to build a log church on the very spot. Thirty years later, settlers erected the current church, a Gothic Revival jewel inside and out.

Christ of the Underworld

Does Christ bless the underworld? He does at John Pennekamp Coral Reef State Park, off Key Largo, Florida. Submerged in twenty-five feet of cyan-blue water is a nearly nine-foot-tall, two-ton bronze statue of *Christ of the Abyss*, or *Christ of the Deep*. Encrusted with barnacles (he's been here since 1965), Christ's arms are held aloft, in a welcoming gesture. While snorkelers can see the statue, divers get up close. They touch Christ's fingertips and bless themselves. They're in holy water, after all.

Landlubbers can visit a replica of the statue (and touch the hem of his garment) at St. Justin Martyr Catholic Church in Key Largo. Standing in a fountain, this statue is also larger than life.

Crucifixion Painting Defies All Odds

Despite calamity after calamity, the centuries-old Crucifixion painting at Saint Mary of the Annunciation Church in Charleston, South Carolina, refuses to give up the ghost. When the large sanctuary painting — executed in 1814 by John S. Cogdell — sustained damage in the Great Charleston Fire of 1838, the local artist repainted the crucified Jesus on the same canvas. Civil War bombardment delivered more church damage, but the painting was spared. Jesus hung on the cross through the Charleston earthquake of 1886, the great hurricane of 1893, and Hurricane Hugo in 1989.

Cat and Mouse Prophecy

Is the end of the world at hand? Not according to a sculpture at Mission San Xavier del Bac, a Spanish Colonial church erected 1783–97, near Tucson, Arizona. Decorating the ornate facade are two cats and two mice. Legend has it the world will end if the cats ever catch the mice. Why the doomsday cats and mice are there nobody knows, but they haven't moved an inch — not through the Civil War, the Great Depression, or the two world wars.

Stamps of Approval

How many American saintly men and women have appeared on United States postage stamps? According to the American Philatelic Research Library in Bellefonte, Pennsylvania, only three, all men. Earning the first "stamp of approval," St. Junípero Serra (1713–1784) graced a forty-four-cent airmail stamp (#C116) in 1985. Born on the Spanish island of Majorca, the Franciscan friar founded nine of California's twenty-one missions, including Mission San Carlos Borroméo de Carmelo at Carmel, where he was buried.

In 1986, the Great Americans series honored Servant of God Edward Flanagan (1886–1948) with his portrait on a four-cent stamp (#2171). The Irish-born priest is best known for opening Boys Town in 1921 near Omaha, Nebraska. A home for wayward and homeless boys, Boys Town — a town in itself — began admitting girls in 1979. Actor Spencer Tracy won an Oscar for his portrayal of Flanagan in the 1938 hit movie *Boys Town*.

Venerable Félix Varela (1788–1853) was hailed as a social

reformer on a thirty-two-cent stamp (#3166) issued in 1997. Born in Cuba, Varela was orphaned at age three and went to live with his grandfather in Florida. Félix returned to Cuba to become a priest. When Father Varela appeared before the Spanish Cortes in 1821 and advocated independence for Cuba and other Spanish colonies, he was marked for execution. The priest fled to New York, where he founded schools, championed civil rights of immigrants, and gained renown as a fiery orator against anti-Catholic bigotry.

Traveling Hermit

Giovanni Maria de Agostini was an oxymoron: a traveling hermit. Born in Italy in 1801, the recluse joined the Maronite church and then set out on a worldwide pilgrimage. The hermit traveled across Europe and South America, living in caves wherever he went. In 1863, the mystic wandered into Council Grove, Kansas, and spent several months in a cave on Belfry Hill, now a park. Later that year, the bearded holy man joined a wagon train on the Santa Fe Trail to New Mexico, traveling the 550 miles on foot.

Agostini found a new cave-home on Hermit Peak, near Las Vegas, New Mexico. Every Sunday, legend holds, he would come down the mountaintop and attend Mass in Las Vegas. The cave dweller soon developed a reputation as a miracle worker, curing people's ailments and once making a spring appear by striking the earth with his staff. To let folks know he was alive and well, he lit a fire at night on the mountain. One night the fire didn't appear. The hermit had wandered on to a new cave, La Cueva, in the Organ Mountains near Las Cruces, in southern New Mexico.

One spring night in 1869, no fire was spotted in the Organ Mountains. Agostini, sixty-eight years old, was found murdered, holding a crucifix and wearing a cilice, an ascetic's spiked iron belt, around his waist. He had worn the spiked belt so long his skin had grown over it. Who murdered the hermit? Why was he murdered? It remains an unsolved mystery.

Mississippi Snow Day

Some people just won't stay put. In 1852, Bishop John J. Chanche, SS, of Natchez, Mississippi, died unexpectedly in Frederick, Maryland. The fifty-six-year-old shepherd had just attended the First Plenary Council in Baltimore. Cholera was the suspected villain of his death.

Mississippi's first bishop, Chanche was buried in Baltimore's Cathedral Cemetery. After twenty-six years of rest, Chanche upped and moved in 1878 to the New Cathedral Cemetery in Baltimore, where he rested for another 129 years. In 2007, the bishop relocated again, this time to Natchez, and even took his grave monument with him. When Chanche was buried for the third time on January 19, 2008, outside St. Mary Basilica, it snowed in Natchez — the first time in over a decade.

Was Our Lady welcoming her son home with the weather spectacle? It was Chanche who had laid the cornerstone in 1842 for Our Lady of Sorrows Cathedral, now St. Mary Basilica.

Daredevil Cathedral

The Cathedral of St. Helena in Helena, Montana, knows a thing or two about daredevils. During World War II, the yarn goes, an air force pilot flew a P-51 fighter plane over the city, buzzing the homes of his mother and girlfriend. Then, on a bet, the foolhardy pilot steered the bird between the twin 230-foot-tall spires of the 1908 Gothic Revival cathedral. He made it, but it's said his guardian angel suffered a clipped wing.

Let's Be Frank

The first Catholic church in Norton, Kansas, was dedicated to the Nativity of Our Blessed Lord. So, why is the church now called St. Francis of Assisi? The answer is "Frank" — lots of Franks.

When Father Richard Daly arrived as pastor in November 1901, there wasn't a stitch of bedcovers to be found in the old, drafty rectory. Daly spent the first night with his overcoat as a blanket and begged his good friend, St. Francis of Assisi — "Frank" if you're on a first-name basis — to round up some bed-covers. Francis, patron saint of the poor, heard the cold man's cry. The very next day Frank Ward delivered a blanket and comforter. Several parish men were named Frank, and Daly's prelate, John Francis Cunningham, had "Frank" in his name.

When the present church was built in 1903, Daly decided to call it St. Francis of Assisi, in honor of all the good Franks. Bishop "Frank" Cunningham officiated at the dedication, of course.

Extreme Trivia QUESTION 19

Our Lady Seat of Wisdom is the patroness of this Catholic college. Students will also find wisdom sitting in the saddle in the college's equestrian program, a required course. Name this college.

Vocations Magnet

There must be something in the holy water at St. Boniface Church in tiny New Vienna, Iowa, population 383. Thirty-four of its men have become priests and more than fifty women have entered religious life. Many big city parishes can't come close to vocation numbers like these. Then again, the spire of the 1884 stone church looks like a giant index finger pointing to God — a sign if there ever was one.

Buffalo Bill and the Pope

In March 1890, Buffalo Bill — America's Wild West icon — made Vatican history. After setting up his Buffalo Bill's Wild West traveling show in Rome, Colonel William F. Cody and his band of cowboys and Indians set off to see Pope Leo XIII at an audience celebrating the twelfth anniversary of his papacy. It's said that Vatican statues turned their heads and gawked as the "savages" with painted faces and tomahawks passed by. The pope blessed Buffalo Bill and his entourage and gave them medals of his pontificate.

Did the papal benediction take? Or was it the influence of the Indians, many of whom were Catholic? For on January 9, 1917, the dying colonel, who had never been baptized, was baptized a Catholic of his own volition at his sister's home in Denver, Colorado. Denver priest and family friend Father Christopher V. Walsh, an Irish native who had seen Cody's show in Europe as a child, administered the sacrament. Buffalo Bill, aged seventy, died less than twenty hours later, his family at his side.

The Wild West legend was laid to rest on Lookout Mountain near Golden, Colorado. One of America's most popular attractions, the Buffalo Bill Museum and Grave holds the papal medal the colonel received during his Vatican visit.

Birds and the Bees

During the 1920s, a pastor at St. Boniface Catholic Church in Sublimity, Oregon, learned about the birds and the bees the hard way. To stop birds from roosting in the ball and cross atop the 100-foot steeple, the priest let fly heavenward a hail of rifle bullets. But the bullet holes in the metal ball only attracted other parishioners: bees. Before long, the German church, erected in 1889 in Carpenter Gothic style, was the "bee-siest" parish in the Willamette Valley.

When the dilapidated ball and cross were replaced in 2011, an exterminator had to be called in to remove a bee nest from inside the ball. Where the bees now attend church, nobody knows.

"Mining" a Church

St. Anne's Church at Columbia, California, is a gold mine inside and out. According to lore, the cornerstone of the historic brick church, built by gold miners in 1856, holds a baking powder tin of gold nuggets and gold dust. The bricks, made of local clay, contain gold. But nothing beats the tale of clandestine mining under the hilltop church. Working by night, the gold miners — some say including the priest himself — dug a tunnel under the church and carried away the pay dirt. During the day, the tunnel opening was covered with rocks and brush. If that wasn't enough church gossip, the angelic painting behind the altar roused more holy suspicion. Painted around 1880 by James G. Fallon, son of a local hotel proprietor, the celestial beings were reputedly modeled after local show girls. "Fallen angels" or not, the painting still graces the church today.

Time Travelers

The Inupiat people of Saint Jude's Catholic Church on Little Diomede Island, Alaska, are time travelers. Little Diomede Island is one of two rocky crags of land located in the middle of the Bering Strait. The other is Big Diomede Island, which belongs to Russia. Less than three miles apart, the two islands are also separated by the International Date Line. When Saint Jude's flock looks across the water to Big Diomede, they're looking to tomorrow. When the time travelers look back at Little Diomede, they've returned to today.

A Bear-y Good Church

Our Lady of the Mountains Church in North Conway, New Hampshire, may be the only American church with a congregation of bears. Yes, bears! On occasion, bears have been sighted at the front doors of the church trying to get in and pray. The church is tucked back in the woods, and signs warn people to be alert for bears. So far, the bears haven't posted signs warning fellow bruins to be on the lookout for humans.

"Sauerkraut Stone"

The first frame Holy Trinity Church at Dresden, North Dakota, was struck by lightning and burned down in 1909. The second frame church caught fire in 1936. The third Holy Trinity Church was built with fieldstones — and a bribe. "The first man in with a load of rocks gets a picnic of beer," Father Christopher Ward told his flock. He also promised that exceptionally pretty or unusual stones would find a position of prominence.

And so it came to pass that a "sauerkraut stone" became a building stone. Placed over a church window, the kidney-shaped stone was practically a family heirloom. It had been used for years by a family to keep the lid on the sauerkraut barrel!

Over time, population dwindled, and Dresden became a ghost town. Closed in 1968, Holy Trinity Church now serves as the "cornerstone" for the Cavalier County Dresden Museum. It remains one of the finest fieldstone churches in America — and possibly the only church with a sauerkraut stone.

What a Pignic!

When Father J. Fred Kriebs arrived in 1924 at St. John the Baptist Church in Peosta, Iowa, he found a mountain of parish debt: $86,500 ($1.5 million in today's dollars). The pastor began visiting his rural flock to discuss ways of lifting the financial burden. Farmers here and there would say, "Don't you want a pig, Father, to help with the debt?" One pig alone was nothing, but after numerous offers of pigs, the priest decided to bring home the bacon. He organized "Pignic Day" and began canvassing the area for pig donations.

On the first Pignic Day in December 1925, over 200 farmers donated an oinker. These piggies were sent to market and sold for $6,000. A year later, on the second Pignic Day, 750 porkers answered the call. The "mortgage lifters" arrived by trucks, in wagons, and even in the back seat of cars, hog-tied. Ten years later, the annual Pignic Day had reduced the parish debt by $67,000 — to $19,500. Father Kriebs was in hog heaven.

Pirate Church

Not every pirate builds a church, but Joseph John Chapman (c. 1787–1849) did. The fantastic tale begins in New England, where Chapman was a shipbuilder. Dreaming of great adventures, one version of the story has it, he went to sea. In 1818, while on a stopover in the Sandwich Islands (Hawaii), Chapman was reputedly shanghaied by privateer Hippolyte Bouchard. Shortly thereafter, Bouchard set his sights on plundering California's missions and ranches. Chapman was captured during a raid near Santa Barbara.

When the Franciscan padres became aware of Chapman's carpentry skills, they put the prisoner to work. "Blonde Joe" constructed a grist mill at Mission San Gabriel Arcángel and a fulling mill, which still stands, at Mission Santa Inés. The padres also tried to convert the young man, "sunk in the darkness of the Baptist faith," as they put it. Where they failed, María Guadalupe Ortega y Sánchez succeeded. In 1822, Chapman was baptized as Juan José, his given name in reverse, and then he married the beautiful María.

Chapman's most notable contribution was to help build the old Plaza Church in Los Angeles. Dedicated on December 8, 1822, Iglesia de Nuestra Señora la Reina de los Ángeles — Our Lady Queen of Angels Church — remains an active parish today. It is surely the only church built by a pirate, shanghaied or not.

Saint Joseph the Postal Worker

Does Saint Joseph deliver mail? He does at St. Joe, Arkansas.

Originally called Monkey Run (land surveyors thought they saw monkeys in trees), the tiny town got its current name around 1900 when six miners from St. Joseph, Missouri, received the most letters at the post office. Now local residents "Go to Joe" to get their mail.

Leave It to Beaver

Sit near a pew end at the Cathedral of St. Joseph in Burlington, Vermont — New England's oldest French Canadian national parish — and you might feel something slapping you. The ends of the old wooden pews are decorated with a beaver-tail pattern (the beaver is the national animal of Canada). A beaver also adorns a ceiling medallion. The parish didn't "leave it to the beaver" to build the church, though. Dedicated in 1887, the church's ornate interior was inspired by the Royal Chapel of the Palace of Versailles at Versailles, France.

Church Whisperer

Don't confess your sins on the "whisper spot" — a floor medallion — in Saint Anselm Abbey Church, located on the campus of Saint Anselm College in Manchester, New Hampshire, or you'll be found out. The support beams of the tall, round roof gather at the top over this spot, creating an echo chamber below. No matter how quietly you whisper, it sounds like you're shouting to the masses. But pray on this spot and heaven will hear you, loud and clear.

Tough Rose Trees

Sacred Heart of Jesus Catholic Church in Tombstone, Arizona — called The Town Too Tough to Die — boasts some mighty tough rose trees. Planted as shoots around 1885, the two Lady Banksia rose trees today are each about five feet around at the base and together provide a canopy of over 2,500 square feet.

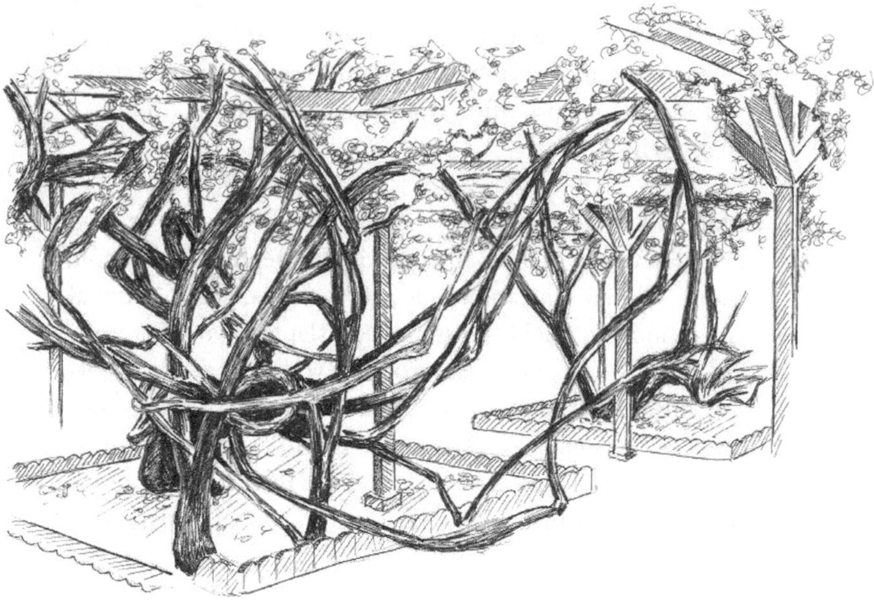

Under the sprawling branches, held up by wooden supports, is the Rose Tree Courtyard — one of the most unique parish gathering spaces in the country.

Big as they are, the historic rose trees with white blossoms are small compared to the World's Largest Rose Tree, also in Tombstone. "The Shady Lady," as it's called, spans 9,000 square feet, and its gnarly trunk is some twelve feet around.

Our Lady of Hallmark

Greetings from Our Lady of Hallmark in Kansas City, Missouri! Employees of the Hallmark greeting card company are known to slip into Our Lady of Sorrows Church — dubbed Our Lady of Hallmark — for prayer and inspiration. The company's headquarters is located directly behind the gorgeous 1920s Italian Renaissance church. It's said the trademark crown on Hallmark cards was inspired by the huge gold crown suspended above the high altar. But Mass goers shouldn't expect greeting-card sermons, unless they go something like this: "Mary, Mary, how can it be? You bore the Savior just for me."

Saint Peter's Gates

If Saint Peter's Pearly Gates in Saint Peter, Minnesota, don't open when you knock, repent and try again. Local Catholic banker Paul Dumdei discovered the tall, ornate metal gates during a trip to Mexico and had them shipped back to the historic river town named for the gatekeeper of heaven. A bit of town levity, the pearly-white gates are illuminated at night for surreal photo ops that are, well, out of this world.

Hunting Miracle at Jump-Off Joe

Father Pius Mutter, pastor of St. Joseph's Church (built in 1905) at Jump-Off Joe, near the tiny town of Valley, Washington, had something to mutter about. During the mid-1950s, the church's altar cross, thurible, sanctuary lamp, and other holy items vanished — stolen! Sunday after Sunday, Mutter begged the thieves to return the hijacked goods. His muttering fell on deaf ears, until one Sunday when he announced that several parishioners had declared "open hunting season" on the thieves. And just like that, the missing items reappeared — proof that God is in the hunting!

Diocese of Chance

The Diocese of Reno, Nevada, was founded by chance. (It couldn't have been Lady Luck because gambling in Nevada wasn't legalized until 1931.) In the 1920s, Cardinal George W. Mundelein, Archbishop of Chicago, was traveling by train through Nevada, when he asked who served as bishop of the vast wilderness expanse. No one, the flabbergasted cardinal learned.

Of the forty-eight states (Alaska and Hawaii were not admitted to the Union until 1959), Nevada was the only state without a diocese.

Mundelein put a "diocesan bug" in the Vatican's ear. The Diocese of Reno was established in 1931 and covered the entire state: 110,540 square miles. The diocese was renamed the Diocese of Reno-Las Vegas in 1976. In 1995, Pope St. John Paul II divided the sprawling diocese in two: the Diocese of Reno for northern Nevada and the Diocese of Las Vegas for the southern end. The Diocese of Las Vegas was elevated to an archdiocese in 2023, and the Diocese of Reno became its suffragan … all because of "chance."

Extreme Trivia
QUESTION 20

Which twentieth-century American cardinal was an avid stamp collector and has a philatelic museum named in his honor?

Holy Monastery!

Petersham, Massachusetts, is spiritually charged. The small town of 1,200 souls is home to three cloistered monasteries, including "his" and "her" Benedictine monasteries. St. Scholastica Priory, a community of Benedictine nuns, arrived in 1985, and St. Mary's Monastery for Benedictine monks followed in 1987. In a Middle Ages tradition rarely seen today, the twin communities (Saints Scholastica and Benedict were twins in real life) reside on the same property, share the same church, and pray the Divine Office together.

The Maronite Monks of Adoration at Most Holy Trinity

Monastery settled here in 1985. Devoted to the adoration of Jesus in the Blessed Sacrament, the black-hooded monks come from a very long monastic tradition — all the way back to Saint Maron, a fourth-century Syriac hermit. The consecration and other prayers and hymns of the Maronite liturgy (an Eastern rite of the Roman Catholic Church) are recited in ancient Syriac Aramaic, the language of Jesus Christ himself.

Tower of Babel

When German-Russian settlers began building Sts. Peter and Paul Catholic Church at Strasburg, North Dakota, in 1910, the younger parish men wanted to spend an extra $1,000 for a taller tower. The brick church was already costing $45,000, so what was another grand? But the church elders, immigrants who remembered collecting and selling buffalo bones for a bit of flour, put the kibosh on that. They feared if the young'uns got their way, they would build another Tower of Babel! The square tower stopped at eighty-five feet.

Stained Glass Bloopers

The Basilica of St. Francis Xavier at Dyersville, Iowa, is known for its fabulous 1889 stained glass windows, including one window that took on a life of its own. When the parish ordered the window of Francis Xavier, the Apostle of the Indies, they wanted their patron saint portrayed as preaching to the "Indians." The artisan blooped and made them Native Americans! Not only that, but the artisan gave the sixteenth-century Jesuit missionary a makeover, updating his hair, mustache, and beard to the style of the late 1880s. Francis Xavier wouldn't recognize himself.

\+ + + + +

"Thou shalt not steal," the Seventh Commandment admonishes.

But who stole the Eighth Commandment ("Thou Shalt Not Bear False Witness Against Thy Neighbor") from St. Edmond Roman Catholic Church in Rehoboth Beach, Delaware? In a triple stained glass window of the Presentation of Christ at the Temple, one side panel shows a burnt offering to God. The other side panel depicts the Ten Commandments in Roman numerals. In an artistic blunder — or was it a warning from the artist? — the Seventh Commandment is repeated twice.

A Matter of Will

When Dutch settlers erected St. Willebrord Catholic Church at Green Bay, Wisconsin, in 1891, they naturally dedicated the High Victorian Gothic temple to St. Willibrord, Apostle to the Frisians. So, why does the church spell Willebrord with an "e" in the middle instead of an "i"? Because stonemasons carved the name wrong. That's not all. The parish nickname isn't St. Willi or St. Wille, but St. Willy. Why not St. Will, pure and simple? Because nobody willed it.

Floating Church

Old St. Mary's Church near Pine Bluff, Arkansas, was a floater. The small wooden building was built in 1782 on a barge at Arkansas Post, a trading post on the Arkansas River. When the river changed course and forced the Post to relocate, St. Mary's went with the flow — up or downriver on the barge — wherever the Post moved. In 1832, the oldest Catholic church in Arkansas was moved from barge to land in Jefferson County.

In 1838, Mother Agnes Hart and her Sisters of Loretto began a school nearby. Mother died the following year of malaria and was buried on a bed of roses (without a coffin). Because the area was prone to flooding, the church and graveyard were moved inland in 1869. When Mother was exhumed for transfer, thirty years after her death, gravediggers gasped: Her body appeared incorrupt. Mother was revered then as a saint and still is today.

Good Church in the Badlands

If you have your own town, why not build your own church? That's exactly what Medora de Vallombrosa, wife of the French Marquis de Morès, did in the picturesque Badlands town of Medora, North Dakota. The Marquis founded the town in 1883 and named it Medora, for his wife. A year later, his devout wife erected St. Mary's Catholic Church — a gift to Medora from Medora. The little yellow brick church even had a touch of class: four pointed windows on each side.

When her husband's beef-packing plant failed in 1886, Medora and family left town. In 1920, Medora's sons deeded St. Mary's Church to the Diocese of Bismarck. The historic church and the Château de Morès remain popular Badlands attractions today.

Gold Rush Relic

How big was the lock and key at St. Joseph's Church in Sawyers Bar, the oldest Gold Rush church in Northern California? Not big enough. The lock, handmade of cast iron, was about one foot square and two inches thick. The key was nine inches long and weighed about one-half pound. How does such a big lock go missing? It's anybody's guess.

St. Joseph's began in 1855, when Father Florian Schwenninger, OSB, persuaded the forty-niners to build a church of whipsawed lumber. The "cornerstone": a corner post with a silver coin bearing the year of the new church. Schwenninger, an Austrian, lived in a lean-to at the rear of the church with his cats and chickens. Years later, when a mining company offered to move the church and graveyard so they could hydraulically blast the land, locals vowed to lynch the first company man to set foot on the church property. The Gold Rush relic still stands as proud as ever.

A Convert's Church

The Shrine of Santa Rita in the Desert at Vail, Arizona, was built by a Catholic convert in memory of a Catholic convert. In the mid-1930s, convert Caroline Takamine Beach erected the small Mission-style adobe church in homage to her first husband, renowned Japanese scientist Jokichi Takamine (1854–1922). A Buddhist, Takamine converted to Catholicism just weeks before his death. The beautiful stained glass windows are converts too, salvaged from a Methodist church. The only Catholic church in America built in memory of a Japanese citizen, the shrine is revered as a symbol of Japanese and American friendship.

A Grave Matter

Four bishops and two archbishops are entombed inside the Cathedral-Basilica of the Immaculate Conception in Mobile, Alabama. Bishop Michael Portier, who laid the cornerstone for the Greek Revival structure in 1835, rests inside. So, why was Bishop John Quinlan, Portier's successor, buried under the portico? It's a grave matter to be sure.

According to one account, Quinlan was buried here because he added the landmark portico in the 1870s. It was a fitting burial spot, people said. But there's another tale that tickles ears. While on his deathbed, Quinlan is reputed to have said, "They walked on me in life, they can now walk on me in death."

Medieval Faces

Old St. Vincent Chapel of Ease, located on the banks of the Mississippi River at Cape Girardeau, Missouri, is a church of many faces — medieval faces. Over 130 plaster faces portraying char-

acters from medieval mystery and morality plays decorate the ends of arches, inside and outside, of the 175-year-old English Gothic church. The faces at Old St. Vincent represent "good and evil" and "youth and old age" — the only known "medieval faces" in the country.

Miracle Water

A miracle is just a prayer away. The Catholic Métis of Pembina County, North Dakota, learned this during a buffalo hunt. In 1862, the Métis, of Indian and European descent, set out for the Missouri River with 100 Red River carts pulled by oxen and ponies. Joining them was Father Jean-Baptiste Genin, who offered daily Mass on the trail. The Métis had just enough food to last them until they reached the hunting grounds. But no buffalo were to be found, and the Métis started for home. With no fresh buffalo meat, they had to kill their oxen and ponies for food.

One day, the Métis told Genin they had no water. Area streams had gone dry. The priest sent them to a lake — near present-day Valley City, North Dakota — but that lake too had dried up. Genin, who had a miraculous way about him, then told the Métis to pray the Rosary and take their kettles back to the lake. To their astonishment, water was bubbling up through cracks in the dry lakebed! The priest offered Mass at the lake and named it St. Mary's Lake. The miracle lake is still filled with water today.

Eccentric Monk Museum

What's football-sized, shaped like a pigskin, and draws tourists like a magnet to the Abbey Museum at Mount Angel Abbey near St. Benedict, Oregon? The world's largest porcine hairball, weighing in at over two pounds. (Let's hope the monks aren't boasting and committing the sin of pride.) It's said the hairball came from a pig grown on the abbey's farm. The eclectic museum also features fossils, antique liturgical vestments and medals, Civil War memorabilia, assorted starfish, rotating artworks, and a menagerie of stuffed animals, including an eight-legged calf and a two-headed cow.

Cow-Pie Church

The first Holy Rosary Catholic Church in Bozeman, Montana, was built in 1885 on the open range: four donated lots enclosed by a fence. To attend Sunday Mass, pioneers had to dodge cow pies and grazing livestock before they reached the church fence, then crawl under the fence and wade through mud or snow to reach the front door. After Mass, they repeated the spiritual exercises in reverse to go home.

In 1907, the current Holy Rosary Church of neo-Gothic design was erected on Main Street. The days of being greeted by moos at Mass were over. The "cow-pie church," however, continues to feed souls. It was moved to Main Street in Bozeman and now serves as a restaurant.

Where Are the Spires?

Go cathedral hopping across the country and you might spot a few cathedrals without spires. What happened to the spires, the crowning glory of cathedrals? Tales of empty coffers.

When Bishop Thomas F. Hendricken began erecting, in 1878, the Cathedral of Saints Peter and Paul in Providence, Rhode Island, he refused to go into debt. He wasn't about to rob Peter to pay Paul. The good bishop died before the Romanesque Gothic church was completed. The spires atop the 156-foot twin towers remain unfinished to this day.

\+ + + + +

The Cathedral of St. John the Evangelist in Boise, Idaho, also suffered from a case of coffer-itis: When money ran out, the towers stopped short. The neo-Romanesque edifice was dedicated in 1921. A throwback to the days when most men wore hats, a wooden column holding up the choir loft once served as the "hat check." Men would hang their hats on hat clips attached to the column before finding their way to a pew.

\+ + + + +

It's a godsend that Bishop (later Archbishop) Jean-Baptiste Lamy — the First Bishop of the Wild West — never had the pesos to construct the steeples atop the Cathedral Basilica of St. Francis of Assisi in Santa Fe, New Mexico. In the 1930s, the Romanesque cathedral was found to be shifting, and steel tie rods were installed and other measures taken to shore up the building. The weight of Lamy's envisioned steeples might have caused the historic cathedral to implode.

Extreme Trivia
QUESTION 21

Which diocese has the Barque of Saint Peter depicted on its coat of arms?

Life in the Saddle

It's a good thing Father Hartig's first name was Emmanuel (God with us). Because the Benedictine pioneer, who spent much of his life on horseback planting churches and stations in southeastern Nebraska, needed God at every turn. Once, he found himself surrounded by hostile natives who, no doubt, intended to scalp him. Hartig reached into his saddlebag and pulled out his black breviary. God was with him. When the natives saw the black book, they thought he was a Black Robe (a Jesuit) and shook his hand.

During the Civil War, God was with Hartig twice. While he was riding horseback in Missouri, Union soldiers arrested him as a spy. After he was released, Confederate soldiers captured Hartig and tried to get him to divulge the number of soldiers and cannons in the Union camp. Hartig didn't cough up any information and was finally sent on his way.

But folks at St. Benedict Catholic Church in Nebraska City, Nebraska, remember the priest-legend every time they look up at the church spire. In 1862, Hartig put a letter documenting the parish history in, of all places, the globe of the cross over the main entrance. The letter was discovered forty-six years later during a church remodel. Thanks to the letter, parishioners know the cost of the original church: $4,000. Compared to today's prices, the church land was a steal: three greenbacks, or three dollars.

Fire-Fighting Cathedral

Not all bells ringing in Little Rock, Arkansas, summoned people to church. When the City of Little Rock acquired a telegraph fire alarm system in 1890, the Cathedral of St. Andrew became a firefighter. When fires broke out, the 3,300-pound bell in the 231-foot bell tower — the tallest in Little Rock — rang out a sequence of bell codes that identified the location of the blaze. The fire alarm bell system was used until 1944.

Building a Church, Pioneer Style

Blood, sweat, and stone: the building blocks of hundreds of pioneer churches. A sign outside St. Lawrence Church in New Hamburg, Missouri, erected in the 1850s, tells the familiar story. "Every family was required to donate $5.00, or deliver eight wagonloads of stone, or take off every tenth day and work on building the church."

When it came time to name the church, however, the Alsatian pioneers quarreled just like the Twelve Apostles, getting into "sainted" arguments. Finally, Wendolin Bucher, who had donated the church land, declared the church would be dedicated to the patron saint of his son, Lawrence. And that was that.

Traveling Organ

Carrying a tune is one thing but an organ? In 1888, the German-speaking flock of Sacred Heart Catholic Church in Glen Ullin, North Dakota, bought a little organ for their little church on the prairie. But nobody knew how to play it. So, the choir leader undertook the task of learning to play the musical instrument — at home. Brawny men would carry the pump organ over to the choir leader's house and then haul it back to church for Mass. If the men couldn't carry a tune, they could an organ.

Grandmother's House

When the cornerstone for the Shrine of St. Anne Catholic Church in Arvada, Colorado, was dedicated on July 4, 1920, Saint Anne had her work cut out for her: More than 800 individual prayer petitions to the saint were placed inside the cornerstone. The shrine, with landmark bell tower, opened in 1922.

Going to "Grandmother's House" (Anne is Jesus' grandmother) soon became a popular Sunday outing — so popular that the dirt road from Denver to Arvada was paved in 1925 to accommodate the heavy traffic, sometimes as many as seventy tin lizzies in one afternoon. How many saints can "pave" a road? Only Good Saint Anne.

Honey of a Church

Why was St. Ambrose Catholic Church in Salt Lake City, Utah, named for a saint with a honeyed tongue? Bee-cause Saint Ambrose is often depicted with a beehive, and bee-cause the beehive is Utah's state symbol. The beehive also represents the Church. A bee works for the swarm and not for himself. He protects the Queen Bee (the Church) and lives in community. According to legend, when Saint Ambrose (c. 339–397) was an infant, his father found the boy's face and lips covered with bees. The bees were taken as a sign that Ambrose would grow up with a honeyed tongue and become a great orator, which he did.

"John Wayne Bishop"

It wasn't easy being a bishop in the Wild West. When Bishop Charles J. O'Reilly, the first ordinary of the Diocese of Baker, Oregon, arrived at his see in Baker City in 1903, four priests were waiting for him — with guns. He wasn't wanted in these parts. According to lore, the Archdiocese of Portland had exiled the malcontent clergy to the wilds of eastern Oregon for "rehabilitation." The renegade priests, however, weren't expecting a "John Wayne Bishop." O'Reilly stuck to his ecclesiastical guns and stayed put.

Holy Oil

St. Patrick Church in Anchorage, Alaska, believes in taking a chance. When the parish needed money to build a multipurpose building in 1977, it launched one of the most creative fundraisers ever: "The Great Alaska Pipeline Classic." People bought five-dollar guesses in the statewide raffle on the number of days, hours, and minutes it would take for the first drop of oil to flow from Prudhoe Bay to Valdez. Purchasers received an official certificate suitable for framing with their guess recorded.

On June 20, 1977, oil started running from Prudhoe Bay. Thirty-eight days later, on July 28, oil reached the Valdez Terminal. The prize for the closest guess: $30,000 ($150,000 today). As it turned out, St. Patrick's was the biggest winner. Raffle proceeds paid for the multipurpose building, which served as the parish worship center until the current church was built in 1996.

"War Rosary"

During World War II, three unrelated parishes in the Midwest began praying the Rosary for their soldiers in harm's way. At all three parishes, every soldier came home alive! The "War Rosary" continued during the Korean and Vietnam conflicts. Again, every soldier lived to tell about it. Amazingly, each parish also has an outdoor grotto dedicated to Our Lady.

St. Mary's Church in St. Benedict, Kansas, erected a grotto before World War II broke out. "I promise you something wonderful if you build a grotto to Our Lady of Lourdes," Father Cyril Bayer, OSB, told his flock in 1936. When America entered World War II on December 7, 1941, parishioners began gathering at the grotto to pray down Mary's mantle of protection over their fathers, sons, brothers, husbands, and boyfriends. Just as Bayer predicted, something wonderful happened. Not one "St. Benedict boy" died in combat.

+ + + + +

The Shrine of Our Lady Queen of Peace at St. John Church in Leopold, Missouri, was dedicated in May 1944, one year before V-E Day. Families would gather at dusk at the "Shrine of Safe Return" and pray their beads for St. John's soldiers on the battlefields. On Memorial Day and Veterans Day, flags line the shrine walkway to honor the soldiers and to give thanks for their safe return — every single one of them.

+ + + + +

A grotto of gratitude, Our Lady of Lourdes at St. Mark the Evangelist Catholic Church in St. Marks (near Colwich), Kansas, was erected after World War II. The grotto holds a plaque with the names of all forty-seven of their soldiers and the Latin words "Deo Gratias" ("Thanks be to God") and "Ave Maria" ("Hail Mary"). Praying it forward, the parish holds a Rosary service on Sunday evenings for the protection of our country.

Prophetic Word

Folks at St. Gabriel Catholic Church in Charlotte, North Carolina, will never forget the first Mass reading on Sunday morning, August 9, 2020. Just minutes after hearing the words from 1 Kings 19:11, "After the wind, an earthquake — but the LORD was not in the earthquake," the earth shook under their feet! The epicenter of the 5.1 magnitude quake was near Sparta, about 100 miles north of Charlotte. It was the most powerful earthquake in the region since 1916.

Streets of Heaven

Take a walk on the heavenly side in Shullsburg, Wisconsin. Venerable Samuel Mazzuchelli, OP (1806–1864), named the streets in the northeast section of the old lead mining town for virtues straight from the Bible. Street names include Faith, Justice, Friendship, Wisdom, Peace, and Goodness, not to overlook Mercy, Charity, Pious, Truth, and Virtue. Oh, don't forget Happy. When townsfolk attend Mass at St. Matthew's Catholic Church, they're reminded of the great hereafter. The church sits on Judgement (yes, "Judgement") Street.

Drive-Through Stations

Come rain or snow, you can always make your Lenten Stations of the Cross at Our Lady of Martyrs Shrine at Auriesville, near Fultonville, New York. Just pray the drive-through stations from the comfort of your car. Wooden posts with stations in relief line both sides of the penitential road. The stations are believed to be the only drive-through stations in the country.

Church of Many Colors

What's in a church name? A story of faith. What's in the exterior color of a church? Most likely a colorful tale.

Some years ago, the pastor of St. Charles Borromeo Church

at St. Francis, South Dakota, part of the St. Francis Mission on the Rosebud Reservation, asked the parish council what color they wanted to paint the church exterior. They got stuck in color limbo and couldn't decide. So, the pastor presented the color chart to the youth group. They picked "Wisteria," a light violet color! It's said the parish council no longer has trouble making decisions in a timely manner.

\+ + + + +

There's no mistaking St. Joseph on the Brandywine Church in Greenville, Delaware: It's yellow. Also called the "DuPont Church," the Delaware landmark was erected in 1841 by DuPont company stone masons — on company time — for Irish and Italian immigrants working in the DuPont powder mills. The Du Pont family also provided for the rectory, convent, and school. Around 1895, Alfred du Pont electrified the church and had it painted the same distinctive yellow as his home. The mustard-like color remains today.

Movers and Shakers

What do five of America's most saintly women have in common? These "movers and shakers" were inducted into the National Women's Hall of Fame at Seneca Falls, New York. St. Elizabeth Ann Seton (1774–1821), founder of the Sisters of Charity, the first religious order for women established in the US, became the first inductee in 1979. Joining her in 1996 was Italian-born St. Frances Xavier Cabrini (1850–1917), founder of the Missionary Sisters of the Sacred Heart of Jesus. Arrested for demonstrating for women's suffrage in 1917, Catholic convert and political activist Servant of God Dorothy Day (1897–1980) became a Hall of Famer in 2001.

A Franciscan sister who helped establish hospitals in New

York and Hawaii and was a pioneer advocate for patient rights, St. Marianne Cope (1838–1918) was inducted in 2005. St. Katharine Drexel (1858–1955), who inherited a fortune and spent it establishing missions and schools for Native and African Americans, was named to the roll in 2011.

Extreme Trivia
QUESTION 22

I am the only American saint with a paid state holiday in my honor. State employees love me. Who am I?

Whopper of a Monstrance

Want to see a "monstrance of a fish"? Visit the Basilica of the National Shrine of the Assumption of the Blessed Virgin Mary in Baltimore, Maryland — Baltimore Basilica for short. Some years ago, a man was fishing in a local reservoir when he thought he had snagged a whopper of a fish. He reeled it in, only to discover the "fish" was a large Gothic monstrance! How the monstrance, with ornate spires, ended up in the reservoir nobody knows. But didn't Jesus tell his apostles — the first fishers of men — to "put out into the deep"?

California Litany

If you said "Pray for us" after reciting the name of every Spanish Catholic town in California, you'd have prayed practically the entire Litany of the Saints. One name for Los Angeles is El Pueblo de Nuestra Señora la Reina de los Ángeles (The Town of Our Lady Queen of the Angels). Pray for us. The first California mission was founded at San Diego. Pray for us. Don't forget the missions at San Juan Capistrano, San Luis Obispo, Santa Clara, and Santa Barbara. Pray for us.

The City of San José honors Saint Joseph and San Francisco, St. Francis of Assisi. Pray for us. The apostles have their own towns too: San Mateo, San Marcos, San Pablo, San Andreas, and San Lucas. Pray for us. Archangels keep watch at San Miguel, San Gabriel, and San Rafael. Pray for us. All ye holy women — Santa Rosa, Santa Monica, Santa Ynez, Santa Paula, and Santa Venetia — pray for us.

Play Ball!

Not even death can stop America's favorite pastime. Buried in New Cathedral Cemetery at Baltimore, Maryland, are four members of the National Baseball Hall of Fame. The cemetery claims more Hall of Famers — all with ties to the Baltimore Orioles baseball team, of course — than any other cemetery in the country. The four gravesites even create an invisible baseball diamond of sorts. At "home plate" is the stately mausoleum of John J. McGraw, inducted into the Hall of Fame in 1937. Joseph J. Kelley (inducted in 1971) rests on first base, Edward (Ned) Hanlon (1996) is interred at second base, and the grave marker of Wilbert Robinson (1945) covers third base.

Saint Who?

In 1930, a 500-pound Sicilian godfather arrived at Holy Family Church in Omaha, Nebraska. He sat on a spectacular gold throne, which took two years to make, and wore a medallion belt encrusted with jewels. The "godfather" was a bronze statue of Saint Alfio, one of three brothers martyred in AD 253 at Lentini, Sicily, for refusing to recant the Faith. Alfio, twenty-two years old and the most outspoken of the trio, had his tongue torn out.

Venerated in only a few American parishes, Alfio enjoyed his annual festivals in Omaha. Aficionados carried Alfio in pro-

cession up and down local streets. One year, they let the saint ride on a gondolier float. Revelers shot cannons filled with confetti, ate Old World foods, and danced the night away. But Alfio, it's said, always had to be back in church by 10:30 p.m. The saint needed his sleep if he was going to work miracles.

When Holy Family Church closed in 2020, Alfio took up residence in Omaha's "Little Italy" at St. Frances Cabrini Church. Alfio still sits on his throne, the spiritual godfather of Omaha.

Life of Riley

When Bishop Charles E. Herzig was named the first bishop of the newly created Diocese of Tyler, Texas, in December 1986, he bought a modest two-bedroom house to live in. Some may have thought the Texas native, the grandson of a Lutheran minister, was headed for the life of Riley. The bishop's residence was located on … Easy Street.

Bishop's Cover-Up

Bishop John J. Hughes may have been the first American bishop to wear a wig. It's said that Hughes, the fourth bishop of New

York, had a parting of the hair while in his forties and began wearing a toupee. History does not record if the good bishop ever had a bad wig day.

Apparently, Hughes never got wind of the 1724 bull issued by Pope Benedict XIII banning clerics from wearing wigs and beards. Back in the day, clerics wore wigs, some with built-in tonsures. The tonsures were made of pigskin or other leather that simulated the color of human skin.

Gone Hunting

When Bishop Henri R. Granjon erected Santa Cruz Catholic Church in Tucson, Arizona, a Spanish Colonial Revival structure with a striking ninety-foot-tall minaret bell tower, he didn't choose the site willy-nilly. It's where the French gastronome — bon appétit — liked to go rabbit hunting!

Wailing Wall

The Wailing Wall at the St. Peregrine Cancer Shrine in Mesa, Arizona, is lined with prayers. Reminiscent of the Wailing Wall in Jerusalem, where Jewish pilgrims for centuries have left written prayers in crevices, pilgrims slip paper prayers into cracks of the fabricated stone wall. Emulating another Jewish custom, some Mesa pilgrims back away from the outdoor wall. It's said not turning your back on the wall symbolizes not turning your back on your prayer to God. The Wailing Wall and St. Peregrine Cancer Shrine are located on the campus of Christ the King Catholic Church.

Turn Up the Heat!

Some graveyard residents at The Historic Church of St. Peter in Brownsville, Pennsylvania, must have thought they had died and gone to heaven: They had heated graves — the only heated graves in the country, according to *Ripley's Believe It or Not.*

As it turns out, the boiler that heated the hilltop stone church was located in a building across the street. The pipes carrying the hot water to the church radiators ran under the cemetery and generated enough heat to melt the snow off several lucky graves.

Section Five

INCREDIBLE LEGENDS AND LORE

Who can resist pious tales and lore? They tantalize the imagination and spark thoughts of the divine. Did a Baby Jesus statue in Michigan really stave off Mexican revolutionaries? Are the bluebonnets in Texas a farewell sign from America's first woman evangelist? Who delivered "pig's food" to nuns at a Utah monastery in their hour of need? All holy legends to be sure.

On the other hand, Saint Urho has a busted halo! In the late 1960s, Pope St. Paul VI replaced the cardinal's galero with a biretta. Is the Red Hat legend the reason why? Do the wild horses on North Carolina's Outer Banks really stop to pray? Was Our Lady of the Fields in Maryland a real apparition, or the whimsy of a young girl's fertile imagination?

Fact or fiction? Truth or whopper? You'll find both in this section featuring incredible legends and lore.

Red Hat Legend

According to tradition, when a cardinal of the Catholic Church dies, his galero — a wide-brimmed, cardinal-red hat with tassels — is hung from the ceiling in his home cathedral. When the galero disintegrates with age and falls to the floor, legend has it, the cardinal's soul is released from purgatory and sails into heaven.

Cardinals John McCloskey (named America's first cardinal in 1875), John M. Farley, Patrick J. Hayes, and Francis J. Spellman — all buried in St. Patrick's Cathedral in New York City — are surely rolling in their crypts. In the 2010s, their deteriorating galeros were repaired and rehung in the ambulatory behind the sanctuary. Will the cardinals ever make it into heaven?

Musical Revenge

Bing Crosby could carry a tune, but did he carry a piano? In 1924, the future media star was a prelaw student at Gonzaga University in Spokane, Washington. One day, according to campus folklore, a music professor told Bing that he was "musically disabled" and would never make it as a musician. Bing took his revenge. When the professor came walking by DeSmet Hall, Bing tossed a piano out of a top-story window. This is why Bing never graduated — he was expelled for the stunt. If the campus legend is true, Crosby must have had a body double. He left the Jesuit school in 1924, and DeSmet Hall, an all-male dormitory, didn't open until a year later — in 1925.

Saint Urho, Superhero

Once upon a time in ancient Finland, grasshoppers as big as jackalopes were threatening the wild grape harvest. Saint Urho (OOR-ho), in a booming voice that reverberated across the land, called out, "*Heinäsirkka, heinäsirkka, mene täältä hiiteen!*" ("Grasshopper, grasshopper, go away!") The vibrations of Urho's words blasted the superbugs into the sea, but not before he could impale one with his mighty pitchfork. In 1982, the Finnish town of Menahga, Minnesota, erected a larger-than-life statue of its patron saint in front of the Menahga Area Historical Museum.

Tourists came by the droves to Menahga, but not Catholic pilgrims. Saint Urho is pure Minnesota myth! Urho was invented in the 1950s, when an Irish department store worker teased his Finnish manager that the Finns lacked a superhero like Saint Patrick, who drove the snakes out of Ireland. So, the Finn invented a grasshopper-exorcising super saint and then one-upped the Irish. He set Urho's "feast day" for March 16, one day before Saint Patrick's Day.

Before long, the cult of Saint Urho began spreading to other Finnish towns in America and even back to Old Finland itself. Everyone loves a saint, even a made-up one.

Extreme Trivia
QUESTION 23

Two decades before I was canonized a saint, I was named an honorary citizen of the United States. Who am I? Hint: I received the Nobel Peace Prize in 1979.

Legendary Holy Horses

The wild horses on North Carolina's Outer Banks are veiled in mystery. How did the Spanish mustangs get here? One tale has it the "Catholic" Banker horses arrived 500 years ago with a Spanish expedition. In 1526, Lucas Vázquez de Ayllón assembled a fleet of five vessels, with two Dominican friars and 650 men and women, to begin a colony in America. The ships carried enough supplies and livestock, including 100 horses, to sustain a settlement. On a hot July day, Servant of God Bartolomé de las Casas blessed the fleet before it departed Hispaniola, thus making everything on board holy.

The flagship *Capitana* was wrecked off the Eastern Seaboard. Were the horses on this ship? Maybe. On September 29 — feast of St. Michael the Archangel — Ayllón founded San Miguel Colony near today's Jamestown, Virginia — eighty years before the English set foot here in 1607. (Another version says the colonists settled at Winyah Bay, near Georgetown, South Carolina.) A friar offered Mass, claimed by some to be the first parish Mass in America. A fever epidemic broke out, killing Ayllón on October 18, and the colony disbanded soon thereafter. Only 150 of the 650 colonists made it back to Hispaniola alive.

But the legendary horses remained, roaming the Outer Banks as free as the wind to this very day. At times, it's said, the herd will stop for what seems like an eternity, standing still as though at prayer. Which of the holy horses determines "prayer time" is as mysterious as the wild horses themselves.

Bishop Carroll's Chair

Bishop John Carroll, SJ (1735–1815), was a celebrated man of "firsts." He was appointed America's first Catholic bishop in 1789 and elevated to first archbishop in 1808. He founded Georgetown University, the nation's first Catholic college, in 1789. Unwittingly, Bishop Carroll also became the subject of a fabled statue — and a chamber pot, of all things.

The yarn begins in 1912, when Georgetown University dedicated the *John Carroll Statue*, located in front of Healy Hall. Mounted atop a granite pedestal, the nearly six-foot-tall bronze sculpture shows the illustrious bishop seated in a chair, his hands resting on the chair arms. In his right hand is a closed book, his index finger marking a page. Prankster students began sneaking out at night and leaving a chamber pot under the bishop's chair. In 1923, a pile of bronze books mysteriously appeared under the chair and the

JOHN CARROLL
FOVNDER

chamber pot pranks became history.

Truth or whopper?

The bishop's statue is real (it has appeared in a number of films), but the chamber pot is a tall tale. The *John Carroll Statue* appears today just as it did when designed by Jerome Connor. The artist modeled the sculpture after the *John Harvard Statue* at Harvard University, a stack of books under Harvard's chair. Even though a sign asks people not to climb the *John Carroll Statue*, graduating students of Georgetown University traditionally crawl up and sit in the good bishop's lap. Oh, the confessions he must hear.

There's one confession John Carroll the Statue did not hear. After thousands of invitations to the 1912 dedication ceremony had been sent out, the foundry informed the university the statue would not be finished in time for the gala event. Rather than cancel the ceremony, school officials ordered a plaster cast made of the statue and painted bronze. Unbeknownst to the huge crowd of dignitaries on hand, the bogus statue was unveiled in all its glory! When the real statue arrived some weeks later, the two statues were switched in the dead of night.

The Farmer and the Nuns

In 1952, a group of five Carmelite nuns in Alhambra, California, answered the call to found the Carmel of the Immaculate Heart of Mary in Salt Lake City, Utah. Concerned about the monastery's temporal needs, Bishop Duane G. Hunt asked each of the nine area parishes to provide the nuns with groceries during their assigned months. One year, during the three-month period when no parish was assigned to deliver food, a man knocked on the monastery door.

"I have an arrangement with a grocery store to haul away their excess food for my pigs," the farmer told them. "But there is more food than my pigs could ever eat." He then offered to give the nuns some of the excess food. The food looked fresh, as though it had been picked fresh that morning.

For three months, the farmer delivered "pig's food" to the monastery. Strangely enough, when the parishes started up again with food deliveries, the man was never seen again.

Poltergeist Nightmare to Retreat Center

If the poltergeist saga near Kearneysville, West Virginia, were made into a movie, people would scream in terror. Around 1794, farmer Adam Livingston, a Lutheran and vehemently anti-Catholic, and his family were living a nightmare: Sounds of horses galloping around their house at night. Burning logs leaping from the fireplace. Cattle mysteriously disappearing. Chickens and turkeys with severed heads. A phantom rope blocking the road up to the Livingston farmstead. Even more bizarre, an invisible pair of shears — known as the Wizard Clip — began cutting crescent shapes in blankets, clothing, tablecloths, even leather shoes.

Protestant ministers tried to evict the evil presence but failed. One day, Livingston had a dream of a man in peculiar robes. A voice said, "He can help you." Livingston went looking for the man and found him: Father Dennis Cahill, a Catholic priest. Despite his hatred of Catholicism, Livingston begged the priest to help him. Cahill blessed Livingston's haunted house with holy water and recited prayers of exorcism. To everyone's utter surprise, a missing sum of family money inexplicably appeared near the priest's feet. The poltergeist activities ceased for a while, then started up again. This time Cahill offered Mass in the home, and peace settled in.

In perhaps the first Catholic revival in postcolonial America, Livingston, his family, and a number of neighbors converted to Catholicism. When Servant of God Father Demetrius Gallitzin arrived at the Livingston farm some months later to investigate the poltergeist story, he was a skeptic. He left a believer. In gratitude for his family's deliverance from evil, Livingston donated over thirty acres of his farm to the Catholic Church. The once-haunted land is now a retreat center, called Priest Field.

Flying Nun

Travel across the American Southwest and you'll notice ubiquitous blue doors on old adobe homes and churches. Some say the doors, ranging in hue from sky blue to turquoise, represent the door to heaven. Others say the blue portals pay homage to early Franciscan friars who began dyeing their gray robes blue to promote belief in the Immaculate Conception of Mary. Devotees of Our Lady of Guadalupe claim the blue color represents Our Lady's mantle.

Still others claim the mystical blue doors commemorate the Lady in Blue — the Spanish mystic Venerable María de Jesús de Ágreda (1602–1665). Wearing a sky-blue cape over her cream habit with black veil, the Franciscan Conceptionist nun bilocated from her cloistered convent in Ágreda, Spain, to the Jumano Indians in what is now West Texas and New Mexico.

During 1620–23, it's claimed the "Flying Nun" visited the Indians over 500 times, walking among them through their land and conversing with them in their own tongue. She even brought them rosaries. María of Ágreda taught the Indians about Christianity and prepared them for baptism. When a band of Indians made the long journey of many sunrises from West Texas to Isleta Pueblo, near Albuquerque, New Mexico, for "the waters," the Franciscan friars were astounded. Where had they learned about baptism? From the Lady in Blue.

Before her last visit to Texas, the nun — the first woman evangelist in America — promised to leave behind a sign of her visits, a sign that would remind the natives to always look to heaven and say their prayers. The sign: a field of bluebonnets, now the state flower of Texas.

Stolen or Not?

The statue of Our Lady of Consolation at St. Augustine Catholic

Church in the hamlet of Leopold, Indiana, tells a stranger-than-not story. During the Civil War, three Union soldiers from St. Augustine's were captured and taken to the Confederate hellhole prison at Andersonville, Georgia. Nearly one-third of the 45,000 prisoners held there died. Staring death in the face, the three soldiers turned to Mary and offered her a deal: If they made it home alive, one of them would travel to their native Belgium and have a replica statue made of Our Lady of Consolation that stood in an ancestral church.

After the war, one of the three men indeed sailed to Belgium to commission a replica of Our Lady's statue. In 1867, the duplicate was enshrined on a side altar at St. Augustine's. Or was it? Another story contends the Civil War veteran couldn't find an artist who could replicate Our Lady's sweet face. Finally, out of frustration, he stole the original statue, sparking an international incident. Belgium's King Leopold II was livid, until he learned the statue was in Leopold, Indiana, a town named for his father, King Leopold I.

What's the real story? Was Our Lady stolen? You'll have to ask her yourself.

Our Lady and the Archbishop

When Archbishop Francis A. Janssens canonically crowned the statue of Our Lady of Prompt Succor in New Orleans, Louisiana, by papal decree on November 10, 1895 — the first papal crowning of a Virgin Mary statue in the US — little did he know that one day he would receive his own crowning of sorts.

On June 9, 1897, Janssens, shepherd of the Archdiocese of New Orleans, and Father Joseph Thebault, chancellor, boarded the steamer *Creole* en route to Holland and France on a trip for the archdiocese. Janssens, who championed devotion to Our Lady of Prompt Succor and knew firsthand that she answered prayers on the double, died of a heart attack during the first twenty-four hours of the voyage. He was fifty-three years old.

According to one account, Thebault begged the ship's captain to return to New Orleans, but the ship had already passed Port Eads, the southern tip of the Mississippi River. Janssens would have to be wrapped in cloth and buried at sea. Distraught, Thebault and fellow passengers entreated Our Lady of Prompt Succor to find a swift way to return Janssens's body to the Crescent City for a proper burial befitting an archbishop.

When Our Lady of Prompt Succor (Quick Help) moves in haste, it's said that you can hear her gown rustle. Did Our Lady's gown ever rustle as she answered this petition! Within hours, the *Hudson*, a ship sailing into New Orleans, met the outgoing *Creole*. The captain of the *Hudson* agreed to transport the archbishop's body back to New Orleans. As his body was being transferred by yawl boat from the *Creole* to the *Hudson*, a rainbow appeared in the sky like a divine arc connecting the two ships. The arc remained until the transfer was completed.

Was the rainbow a mirage? The figment of a writer's fertile imagination? Hardly. Everyone aboard the two ships witnessed

the "miracle at sea." A few days later, *The Times-Picayune* of New Orleans carried a story on Janssens's death and the otherworldly rainbow.

Though 130 years have passed, Our Lady and the "rainbow crossing" hasn't faded from local Catholic history. A painting of the celestial event, executed in 1898 by Ursuline Sister Ste. Helene Forstall, adorns the Ursuline Convent Museum at Ursuline Academy in New Orleans. Crowned by papal decree, the statue of Our Lady of Prompt Succor graces the National Votive Shrine of Our Lady of Prompt Succor, also in New Orleans.

Prophetic Bell

Ring the old bell at San Miguel Chapel in Santa Fe, New Mexico — the country's oldest extant church erected between 1610 and 1626 — and you might be prophesying your future. Legend holds if you ring the 780-pound bell, housed inside the adobe chapel, long enough, the spirits will return you to Santa Fe. Some claim the bell, inscribed in relief with "*San Jose Rogad Por Nosotros Agosto 9 de 1356*" ("Saint Joseph, pray for us, August 9, 1356") was cast in Spain in fulfillment of a vow. As the tale goes, villagers of San José, in the Andalusia region of southern Spain, were desperate to expel the Moors from their land. They promised Saint Joseph to christen a bell in his name if he pushed them back. The Moors were driven out during the very next battle.

Others say the bell was cast in New Mexico in 1856, the "3" a flaw in workmanship.

The date didn't matter to an old blind man who would visit the chapel every day at noon to pray the Angelus. Tapping and feeling his way to the altar rail, he would drop to his knees and invoke Saint Cecilia, patron of music. Miraculously, the bell would begin "singing," and the old man could see everything in the chapel: the Spanish Colonial reredos, the wooden statue of

St. Michael the Archangel with silver sword, the old wooden vigas in the ceiling. When the pealing stopped, the man went blind again — until the next day when he came back to pray.

Extreme Trivia QUESTION 24

I am called the "Prince of American Architecture" because I designed over 600 American Catholic churches, including at least sixteen cathedrals. Chances are, you've visited one of my churches.

Crucifixion Mystery

The Crucifixion painting at Yellow Fever Martyrs Church and Museum in Holly Springs, Mississippi, is steeped in mystery. One Saturday in 1858, the common version of the story goes, a traveler dressed in medieval clothing arrived at St. Joseph's Church, as the church-museum was then called. He asked the itinerant priest, who was cleaning the church for Sunday Mass, if he could rest a spell. The priest gave the stranger food and let him stay in the small bedroom shed at the back of the church.

Before the priest left, the traveler promised to create a religious painting for the church in gratitude for the priest's hospitality. The priest nodded in appreciation but doubted the promise would come to pass. Besides, the traveler didn't have any art materials with him. When the priest returned a few weeks later, he found a painting of Christ's crucifixion inside the bedroom shed. He asked the neighbors if they had seen the stranger or witnessed the painting's creation, but no one had seen or heard a thing. The stranger had simply vanished.

At the bottom of the painting are the Latin words "*A. F. Michelly, fecit A.D. MDCCCLVIII*" ("A. F. Michelly had this made in the Year of Our Lord 1858"). In the late 1850s, Alexander F. Michelly was a professor of painting at Franklin Female Institute in Holly Springs. He died in Natchez, Mississippi, in 1860.

Was Michelly the stranger? Or did the stranger hire Michelly to paint the artwork? If the stranger was indeed Michelly, why was the professor dressed in old clothes? And why did he stay in the bedroom shed since he lived in Holly Springs? Who was the mysterious traveler? Did the priest entertain an angel unaware?

In Michelly's portrayal of the crucifixion, Jesus is nailed to the cross with four nails (not the usual three nails), his eyes searching heaven, "My God, my God, why have you forsaken me?" The mysterious painting still baffles people to this day.

Our Lady of the Fields

Once upon a time, in 1642 to be exact, a Piscataway Indian chief in southern Maryland named Ottawanta and his family were baptized into the Catholic Faith. Ostracized by the tribe for their new religious beliefs, the chief and his family migrated to northern Maryland and settled near present-day Emmitsburg. One by one Ottawanta's family died — his wife, five sons, and one daughter. The chief planted an oak tree over each grave, much like a marker in a cemetery.

All alone in his adopted land, Ottawanta would visit the circle of oak trees daily, pray his rosary beads, and beg to die. One day, the Blessed Mother appeared to the pious Indian and said, "My son, here I am. I have heard thy prayer. I have counted thy fervent Aves of sixty summers, repeated on this spot; now I give thee a pledge of my love and of thy fidelity to me. Soon my son, thou wilt join thy children [and thy wife] far above the skies, but this spot will forever bear testimony to thy love and fidelity to me."

Ottawanta's countenance brightened as Our Lady continued.

Here on this holy mountain "a temple dedicated to my name will crown the mountain's brow, where innumerable bands of Levites and mitered heads will depart to convey the tidings of the Gospel over the wide-spread world. ... A holy sisterhood will arise, and souls consecrated to the Lamb will repair hither and repeat Aves that will not give back their echo to the wild, but will be answered by a thousand voices. ... Here I will be honored as the Flower of the Field and the Lily of the Valley."

Before seven suns had set, Ottawanta fell ill and soon joined his family in the Land of Everlasting Happiness.

Our Lady's prophecy came to pass in 1806, when French refugee Father Jean DuBois erected St. Mary's Chapel on the Hill (now the National Shrine Grotto of Our Lady of Lourdes). Two years later, he founded today's Mount St. Mary's University and Seminary. Many mitered heads indeed came forth from this holy mountain, just as Our Lady had foretold, including DuBois, who became bishop of New York in 1826. In 1809, Mother Elizabeth Ann Seton settled at Emmitsburg and founded both the Sisters of Charity of St. Joseph and St. Joseph's Academy, a school for girls.

Over the years, the saga of Our Lady's visits to Ottawanta appeared in a number of Catholic magazines and books and on websites as a historical account. A sign near the apparition site even gave a detailed report of the fascinating event.

Why hasn't this apparition garnered more attention and prominence? Because it's pure fantasy! As the story goes (literally), Mary Elizabeth Smith (1813–1884), a student at St. Joseph's Academy in the 1820s, invented the legend as a creative writing composition. The clever girl would have known about the founding of the seminary and of Mother Seton's religious order. Smith later entered the Sisters of Charity (now called the Daughters of Charity), took the name Sister Mary Raphael, and eventually became directress of St. Joseph's Academy.

Her legendary story, held in the archives of the Daughters of Charity at Emmitsburg, is still making the rounds, as a matter of fact.

Miracle of the Swallows

Only the birds know the real story of the legendary return of the swallows around March 19 — feast of Saint Joseph — to Mission San Juan Capistrano, in the southern California town of San Juan Capistrano.

On March 19, 1777, one story flies, an old Indian man was on his way to Mass at the new mission when he saw several cliff swallows circling overhead. The birds disappeared as quickly as they came. When Mass was over, the Indian stepped outside. The swallows had returned with thousands more of their kind. On October 23 — feast of St. John of Capistrano, the mission's namesake — the birds took wing for the winter. The swallows returned every March 19, as though they had calendars. Leap years didn't seem to interrupt their flight plans.

Or did the tradition begin with Father St. John O'Sullivan, mission pastor from 1910 to 1933? According to mission lore, the priest was walking through town one day, when he happened upon a shopkeeper, broom in hand. He was knocking down the swallows' mud nests from under the shop's eaves.

"What in the world are you doing?" O'Sullivan asked.

"I'm getting rid of these nuisance birds," the shopkeeper replied.

O'Sullivan called out to the birds, "Come, my swallows. I will give you shelter at the mission. There's room enough there for all."

The very next morning the priest, whose birthday just happened to be March 19, found swallows building nests at the mission. And so, every feast of Saint Joseph, the mission celebrates the return of the swallows with a fiesta. Come October 23, the town bids adios to their winged friends, as the birds fly off to their wintering grounds in Argentina, 6,000 miles south.

Miraculous Staircase

When the Loretto Chapel in Santa Fe, New Mexico, was nearing completion in 1878, the Sisters of Loretto noticed a glaring defect: There was no staircase to the choir loft! The sisters were in a "staircase pickle." Because the choir loft was so high, there

wasn't room for a regular staircase. And climbing a ladder would be perilous for the sisters in their long black dresses. What to do? The good sisters began a novena to Saint Joseph, patron of carpenters.

On the final day of the novena, the story goes, a bearded, gray-haired man knocked on the convent door. "I've come to build a staircase," he told Mother Magdalen Hayden, the convent superior. Armed with a hammer, a saw, a T-square, and a few hand tools, the stranger erected an exquisite staircase of wood. Making two 360-degree turns, the thirty-three-step staircase appears to be floating on air: There is no center support or load-bearing column. Instead of nails, only square wooden pegs were used. Even more amazing, it's said the wood is of an unknown origin.

Who was the mysterious carpenter who disappeared before he could be paid? Many believe it was St. Joseph the Carpenter who had come to answer the sisters' prayers.

Nature's Crosses

Even nature echoes the crucifixion story. According to legend, fairies were dancing 2,000 years ago in the merry foothills of Virginia's Blue Ridge Mountains, when an elfin messenger brought word of Jesus' death on the cross. The fairies began to weep tempestuously, their falling tears crystallizing into little stone crosses, which then disappeared into the earth.

As time passed, the crosses — known as fairy stones or fairy crosses — worked their way to the surface at Fairy Stone State Park near Stuart, Virginia, one of the few places in the world where fairy crosses are found. The crosses, typically one-half-inch long, come in three distinct Roman Catholic shapes. Saint Andrew's crosses are X-shaped, Roman crosses resemble a plus sign, and Maltese crosses have arms of equal length.

Park visitors come to hunt for their own fairy crosses —

which are actually staurolite crystals, a naturally occurring phenomenon through which Mother Nature participates in the story of our redemption.

Miracle Baby

Jesus saves, even as an infant. In the early 1910s, the pious legend goes, Mother Mary Elias Thierry, a Mexican Carmelite nun, was traveling by train in Mexico. Because Mexican revolutionary soldiers were arresting Catholic religious, the nun was disguised as a housewife. As part of her housewife persona, the thirties-something nun carried in her arms a statue of the sleeping Infant Jesus snuggled in a blanket, just like a real baby.

Also aboard the train were revolutionary soldiers, making their way from one train car to the next. One soldier, notorious for spotting religious in disguise, noticed the housewife and her little bundle. "That baby is awfully quiet," he said, and started toward Mother. At that very instant, the Infant Jesus statue began to wail like a real baby! The soldier retreated and left Mother alone.

Reminiscent of the Holy Family's flight into Egypt, Mother, her little band of Carmelite sisters, and the Infant Jesus statue fled Mexico for their very lives. In 1916, Mother founded the Discalced Carmelite Monastery of Our Lady of Guadalupe at Grand Rapids, Michigan (now located in nearby Ada). Wrapped in a blanket, the Infant Jesus statue has been known to cry, blush, and even coo like a baby.

Converting Adam and Eve

It was only a matter of time before Adam and Eve became Catholic. It happened in 1863 at St. Mary in the Mountains Catholic Church in Virginia City, Nevada. According to Wild West lore, an old Paiute Indian chief began frequenting the church (the current Gothic edifice was built after the Great Fire of 1875) and became enamored with the painted Stations of the Cross. Day after day, the septuagenarian would walk the stations, pausing at each one in deep contemplation.

One day Father Patrick Manogue, the legendary gold miner-turned-priest, happened to walk through the church during the chief's visit. The chief asked Manogue what the pictorial stations meant. The old Indian was so moved by the story of Christ's Passion that he asked to baptized. Some weeks later, Manogue baptized the chief and his wizened wife and christened them Adam and Eve. Chief Adam then brought his descendants, to the fourth generation even, to St. Mary's, and all were baptized.

And that's how Adam and Eve came to be Catholic.

Extreme Trivia
QUESTION 25

Why do devils hate round churches?

Five Betrayals of Judas

When Italian artist Rosa Caselli Moretti accepted the commission to recreate Leonardo da Vinci's Last Supper in stained glass, she couldn't have fathomed that Judas would betray her. It was as though she and the fallen apostle were slugging it out in a spiritual battle.

It began in 1924, when Hubert L. Eaton of Forest Lawn Memorial Park in Glendale, California, asked the stained glass artist of the Moretti Casselli Studio in Perugia, Italy — renowned for its artistic windows in Italian cathedrals and churches — to make a life-size replica of the Last Supper in stained glass. Moretti replied, "I will not copy the Last Supper in Milan, as it is no longer

Leonardo's. I will use the original sketches so when finished it is a reproduction of the original painting, precisely as it was when Leonardo laid down his brushes so long ago."

It took Moretti seven years to complete the stained glass window, three years longer than it took da Vinci to paint his masterpiece. Something otherworldly kept happening: The figure of Judas, the betrayer of Jesus (and now of Moretti the artist), kept breaking during the firing process. Five times this happened. Moretti informed Eaton about the delay, adding, "If Judas breaks again, I shall not finish the Last Supper."

Moretti prayed and tried again. Some weeks later, Eaton, a Baptist known for commissioning replicas of many Catholic works of art, received a telegram: "The Last Supper is finished!" The battle was over. Eaton and all of Catholic Italy, who knew about the mystical war, breathed a collective sigh of relief. Jesus was victor once again!

Did Moretti receive divine intervention to complete the work? Nobody knows, but the stained glass window, which dominates one wall in the Great Mausoleum at Forest Lawn Memorial Park, is a wonder to behold. Spanning thirty feet wide and fifteen feet high (the size of da Vinci's painting), the colors are spectacular. And Judas — well, he hasn't cracked or moved an inch.

ANSWERS TO EXTREME TRIVIA QUESTIONS

1. I am Blessed Miriam Teresa. I was born Teresa Demjanovich on March 26, 1901, at Bayonne, New Jersey. In 1925, I entered the Sisters of Charity of Saint Elizabeth at Convent Station, New Jersey, and took the name Miriam Teresa. My health began to fail, and I passed into God's hands on May 8, 1927, at age twenty-six. My Beatification Mass — the country's first — was held October 4, 2014, at the Cathedral Basilica of the Sacred Heart in Newark, New Jersey. My remains are interred in the Motherhouse Chapel at Convent Station.

2. Leoville, Kansas, honors Pope Leo XIII and is possibly the only town in America named for a then-living pope. The German pioneers also built Immaculate Conception of the Blessed

Virgin Mary Church, a local Romanesque landmark.

3. If you stacked six-foot-tall men, one on top of the other, you would need eleven men to change a ceiling light bulb in the Cathedral Basilica of St. John the Baptist at Savannah, Georgia. Fortunately, the cathedral architects had a brighter idea: The lightbulbs are changed via a catwalk inside the attic.

4. My name is Bishop (later Archbishop) John Baptist Purcell, and I am the bishop maker. On May 20, 1841, I laid the cornerstone for the Cathedral of St. Peter in Chains at Cincinnati, Ohio, and consecrated no fewer than fourteen bishops within these sacred walls. The "bishop factory" was elevated to a basilica in 2020.

5. This French newspaper ad was recruiting missionary priests for America. It's hard to believe, but priests responded. They are among the many unsung Catholic heroes of our land.

6. There are twenty-two — not twelve — islands in the Apostle Island archipelago, and not one island is named for an apostle. It's believed that early French Jesuit missionaries discovered the islands and named them "the Apostles." It's not known if the Jesuits actually counted the islands before bestowing the name.

7. The Basilica of Saint Peter is located in Columbia, South Carolina, and is known as the "Mother Church of the Midlands." Buried in the 200-year-old church graveyard is centenarian Hugh McElrone. Born in Ireland on November 2, 1798, McElrone lived in three centuries — eighteenth, nineteenth, and twentieth — before expiring on December 20, 1901, at age 103.

8. My Trappist name was Louis. My grave marker reads, "Fr. Louis Merton, Died Dec. 10, 1968."

9. In the 1960s, St. Elizabeth Ann Seton's former home at 8 State Street in New York City had to be razed. Up went Our Lady of the Rosary Church (also called the Seton Shrine), designed in a hybrid Federal-Georgian style. It's said that architects Walter Knight Sturges and Joseph Sanford Shanley, a descendant of Mother Seton, wanted the interior to be reminiscent of a ballroom in honor of the saint, who loved to dance.

10. The three dioceses that converge at the Four Corners Monument are Salt Lake City (Utah), Pueblo (Colorado), and Gallup (Arizona-New Mexico — the Gallup diocese straddles both states). Sorry, no indulgences given for praying in three dioceses at once.

11. I am Venerable Fulton Sheen (1895–1979), the nation's first televangelist, according to a 1952 cover story in *TIME* magazine. When Ramón Antonio Gerardo Estévez had trouble landing acting jobs, he invented the stage name Martin Sheen and became a movie star. My remains are entombed in the Cathedral of St. Mary in Peoria, Illinois; the nearby Archbishop Fulton Sheen Museum holds my TV props and other artifacts.

12. The football team was the New Orleans Saints, and the composer of the prayer was Archbishop Philip M. Hannan. It took forty-two years for the prayer to kick in, though. The Saints won their first Super Bowl in 2010.

13. The Alamo, the oldest of five Spanish colonial missions at San Antonio, Texas, was founded in 1718 as Mission San Antonio de Valero — for St. Anthony of Padua and the Marqués de Valero. Six years later, the mission moved to its present location. In 1883, the Diocese (later Archdiocese) of San Antonio sold the Alamo church to the State of Texas.

14. Brides who dream of walking the longest aisle of any American Catholic church on their wedding day should reserve the Cathedral of Mary Our Queen in Baltimore, Maryland. The aisle is 165 feet long, nearly half the length of a football field.

15. The five slain missionaries are known as the Five Martyrs of Georgia. Mission Santa Catalina de Guale on St. Catherines Island was "lost" to history until the 1970s when archaeology excavations began. In addition to holy medals, crosses, and a figurine of the Infant Jesus, the bodies of some 432 Guale Indians were found buried under the remains of the old mission church.

16. I am Sister Thea Bowman (1937–1990), born in Yazoo City, Mississippi. Raised a Methodist, I was nine years old when I became Catholic. At age fifteen, I joined the Franciscan Sisters of Perpetual Adoration at La Crosse, Wisconsin, and became the order's first black sister. In 1989, while addressing the US bishops on black spirituality, I led them in singing the gospel hymn "We Shall Overcome." The bishops not only swayed to the music, but many had teary eyes from the power of the moment. The Diocese of Jackson, Mississippi, is handling my cause for canonization.

17. The roll of the dice on the coffered ceiling of the Cathedral of the Incarnation is scriptural and represents the soldiers who cast lots for Jesus' clothing at Calvary. Other images symbolize Jesus' incarnation and crucifixion, including a shepherd's crook with a cross.

18. I am Father Pierre-Jean De Smet, SJ, and I am featured in a twenty-by-fifteen-foot corn mural at the World's Only Corn Palace in Mitchell, South Dakota. My black robe is done up in black ears of corn, and I'm shown blessing the Badlands, constructed of corn ears ranging in color from yellow to brown to black. I'm grateful that my mural is located inside the Corn Palace, or the birds would have pecked me to death — martyred for the Faith.

19. Saddle up if you want to attend Wyoming Catholic College at Lander, Wyoming. Every sophomore student spends a semester learning the basics of horse care and saddling. They also hone their riding skills so they can take part in a quadrille formation. Graduates of the college are bestowed with — what else — a black Stetson cowboy hat.

20. Cardinal Francis J. Spellman began collecting stamps during his seminary days in Rome in the early 1910s. He once said, "Stamps are miniature documents of human history." The prelate's collection of miniature documents — upward of 10,000 stamps — is housed in the Spellman Museum of Stamps and Postal History at Regis College in Weston, Massachusetts.

21. The Barque of Saint Peter sails on the coat of arms for the Diocese of Salt Lake City, Utah. Salt Lake City borders the Great Salt Lake, often called America's Dead Sea.

22. I am Mother Frances Cabrini, and the State of Colorado celebrates my life on Frances Xavier Cabrini Day, the first Monday in October. Cabrini Day was signed into law in 2020, making me the first American saint with a paid state holiday.

23. You can call me Mother Teresa or St. Teresa of Calcutta. In 1996, I was made an honorary citizen of the United States, only one of two people bestowed the honor while alive. The other living recipient was Sir Winston Churchill, who became an honorary citizen in 1963.

24. I am Patrick C. Keely (1816–1896). During my fifty-year career, I designed an average of twelve churches per year. Many people consider my prolific building — from Maine to Louisiana — all the more amazing because I had no formal training as an architect.

25. Devils are terrified of round churches because there's no place to hide! You won't find any devils hiding inside Saints Peter and Paul Church at Cary, Illinois. Not only is the church round, but the circular wall of color glass blocks lights up like a divine kaleidoscope.

INDEX BY STATE

The page numbers at the end of each entry in this index refer to the page on which that place is mentioned.

ALABAMA

ALASKA

ARIZONA

ARKANSAS

CALIFORNIA

COLORADO

CONNECTICUT

DELAWARE

DISTRICT OF COLUMBIA

FLORIDA

GEORGIA

HAWAII

IDAHO

ILLINOIS

INDIANA

IOWA

KANSAS

KENTUCKY

LOUISIANA

MAINE

MARYLAND

MASSACHUSETTS

MICHIGAN

MINNESOTA

MISSISSIPPI

MISSOURI

MONTANA

NEBRASKA

NEVADA

NEW HAMPSHIRE

NEW JERSEY

NEW MEXICO

NEW YORK

NORTH CAROLINA

NORTH DAKOTA

OHIO

OKLAHOMA

OREGON

PENNSYLVANIA

RHODE ISLAND

SOUTH CAROLINA

SOUTH DAKOTA

TENNESSEE

TEXAS

UTAH

VERMONT

VIRGINIA

WASHINGTON

WEST VIRGINIA

WISCONSIN

Crosse, WI 54601. (608) 782-5610. fspa.org, sistertheabowman.com. **(51, 220)**

Green Lake Conference Center: W2511 State Road 23, Green Lake, WI 54941. (920) 294-3323. glcc.org. **(70)**

Miracle Tabernacle: Peshtigo Fire Museum (Memorial Day–October 8), 400 Oconto Avenue, Peshtigo, WI 54157. (715) 582-3244. peshtigofiremuseum.com; St. Mary's Church (October 9–Memorial Day), 171 South Wood Avenue, Peshtigo, WI 54157. (715) 582-3876. stmaryjosephedwardparish.org. **(104)**

National Shrine of Our Lady of Champion: 4047 Chapel Drive, Champion, WI 54229. (920) 866-2571. championshrine.org. **(17–18)**

St. Joan of Arc Chapel: Marquette University, 1250 West Wisconsin Avenue, Milwaukee, WI 53233. (414) 288-6873. marquette.edu/st-joan-of-arc-chapel. **(26–27)**

St. Lawrence Church in Stangelville: N2085 County Road AB, Denmark, WI 54208. (920) 863-8747. friendsofstlawrence.org, stthereseonline.com. **(163–164)**

St. Matthew's Catholic Church: 344 North Judgement Street, Shullsburg, WI 53586. (608) 776-4059. stisidorewi.org, experienceshullsburg.com. **(189)**

St. Willebrord Catholic Church: 209 South Adams Street, Green Bay, WI 54301. (920) 435-2016. stwillys.org. **(178)**

WYOMING

Diocese of Cheyenne: 2121 Capitol Avenue, Cheyenne, WY 82003. (866) 790-0014, (307) 638-1530. dcwy.org. **(150, 158)**

St. Patrick's Catholic Church: 400 Country Club Road, Casper, WY 82609. (307) 235-5535. stpatricks-casper.com. **(158)**

Wyoming Catholic College: 306 Main Street, Lander, WY 82520. (877) 332-2930. wyomingcatholic.edu. **(221)**

INDEX OF NOTED PEOPLE IN CATHOLIC AMERICA

C

D

I

J

K

L

M

N

O

P

U

V

W

Z

ACKNOWLEDGMENTS

It would be impossible to acknowledge each and every person who helped with this book. To begin, there are the church historians of decades and centuries past who had the foresight to document their parish histories and lore. Their observations are not only amusing at times but give us latter-day Catholics a glimpse into the enormous sacrifices that our forefathers made on the frontiers of Faith. May God rest their souls.

Special accolades must also be given to present-day pastors, parish staffs, and diocesan archivists who tracked down details or offered story suggestions. The art of storytelling is one of the oldest forms of communication — an art form used by Jesus Christ himself. May heaven reward you many times over ... with more stories, of course.

ABOUT THE AUTHOR

America's Catholic storyteller Marion Amberg is known for her engaging writing style, sense of humor, and knack for sniffing out the untold story. When it comes to storytelling, her motto is "No trivia is too trivial!" In addition to *Incredible Catholic America: Smallest, Tallest, Oldest, Oddest,* Amberg is the author of two award-winning Catholic travel guides, also from OSV. The author's storytelling days began on the family farm in Minnesota, when she was often placed in charge of younger siblings. The only way to keep the brood entertained was to tell stories and take them to "distant lands" — to a hollow in the cow pasture or to a patch of virgin prairie to pick wildflowers. Every story, every "trip" became an adventure. In due time, Amberg began freelance writing, taking readers on trips to "distant lands" across America. Her feature articles, mainly human interest and travel pieces, have appeared in over 100 markets around the country.